"This book immediately affected the way I had conversations with my grand-children about some teachable moments in their lives. Smith brings together Scripture and illustrations in a way that makes you want to do better in those conversations, and helps you know how to do it."

Ed Welch, Faculty and Counselor, Christian Counseling & Educational Foundation

"If you're like me, you might have read the title of this book, *Parenting with Words of Grace*, and felt the need to stifle a moan. *Oh, no . . . here comes the guilt!* Please don't make that assumption. Like its title, this book is filled with words of grace: grace to you as a parent and grace to you as a child of the only Father who knows what it is to always speak with words of grace. It's full of deeply satisfying encouragement for your soul and is written in a winsome and honest way. You'll be glad you read it. You really will."

Elyse Fitzpatrick, author, *Give Them Grace*

"A rich resource loaded with scriptural insight. Bible lovers will relish Smith's use and application of Scripture. Parents will be comforted that they are not alone in some of their struggles and given helpful instructions on how to be good parents."

Ajith Fernando, Teaching Director, Youth for Christ, Sri Lanka; author, *The Family Life of a Christian Leader* and *Discipling in a Multicultural World*

"*Parenting with Words of Grace* delivers on its title. In short, easy-to-read chapters, Bill Smith introduces parents to God's amazing grace for their own lives and helps moms and dads understand how to apply that grace in their families. The wisdom found in these pages will help you love your kids in spite of their failures, trust God for the outcome of your parenting, and en-courage your children through the trials they face."

Marty Machowski, Executive Pastor, Covenant Fellowship Church, Glen Mills, Pennsylvania; author, *Parenting First Aid* and *Long Story Short*

"I am allergic to formulaic, pedantic, 'how-to' Christian books on parenting. Thankfully, that is *not* what this book is. Bill Smith recognizes that gospel-shaped parenting is more like art than mathematics; we need to depend more on the Holy Spirit than any how-to manual! Most importantly, Smith urges Christian parents to see their God-given role as authoritative, yes, but also formative as they use their *words* and *conversations* to establish a Christ-centered relationship with their children that can continue for all eternity. I commend this book to you and have already benefited from it myself."

Jon Nielson, Senior Pastor, Spring Valley Presbyterian Church, Roselle, Illinois; coeditor, *Gospel-Centered Youth Ministry*

"Who doesn't want to invite their children into a healthy, vibrant relationship? I know I do. Bill Smith gives a compelling vision for how our words and conversations shape our parenting and how, through our words, we are vehicles through which our children see God. I read this book and wanted to go talk to my kids. You will too."

Courtney Reissig, author, *Glory in the Ordinary*

"A powerful and encouraging read! Bill Smith highlights the power of our words as motivators for our children to seek a real and lasting relationship with Jesus Christ. He offers encouragement for our failed words and help for our future words."

Shona Murray, author, *Refresh: Embracing a Grace-Paced Life in a World of Endless Demands*

Parenting with
Words of Grace

Parenting with Words of Grace

Building Relationships with Your Children
One Conversation at a Time

William P. Smith

Foreword by Paul David Tripp

WHEATON, ILLINOIS

Trade paperback ISBN: 978-1-4335-6097-2
ePub ISBN: 978-1-4335-6100-9
PDF ISBN: 978-1-4335-6098-9
Mobipocket ISBN: 978-1-4335-6099-6

Library of Congress Cataloging-in-Publication Data

Names: Smith, William Paul, author.
Title: Parenting with words of grace : building relationships with your children one conversation at a time / foreword by Paul David Tripp ; William P. Smith.
Description: Wheaton, Illinois : Crossway, 2019. | Includes bibliographical references and index.
Identifiers: LCCN 2018034119 (print) | LCCN 2018051459 (ebook) | ISBN 9781433560989 (pdf) | ISBN 9781433560996 (mobi) | ISBN 9781433561009 (epub) | ISBN 9781433560972 (trade paperback) | ISBN 9781433561009 (epub) | ISBN 9781433560996 (mobipocket)
Subjects: LCSH: Parent and child—Religious aspects—Christianity. | Parenting—Religious aspects—Christianity. | Oral communication—Religious aspects—Christianity.
Classification: LCC BV4529 (ebook) | LCC BV4529 .S65 2019 (print) | DDC 248.8/45—dc23
LC record available at https://lccn.loc.gov/2018034119

Crossway is a publishing ministry of Good News Publishers.

BP			29	28	27	26	25	24	23	22	21	20	19
15	14	13	12	11	10	9	8	7	6	5	4	3	2	1

To Cassie, Timmy, and Danny,
you've added so much to my life and to this book—
without you, both would be far less rich.

Contents

Foreword

Some books are informative, and sometimes new information can change our lives. Some books confront, and sometimes we need someone to interrupt our private conversations to help us see ourselves with more accuracy and evaluate our behavior more humbly. Some books give hope. We all know that sometimes hope is hard to find, and because it is hard to find, joy is difficult to experience. And when you have no joy, it's hard to be motivated to do the uncomfortable things that we all have to do in this fallen world. What I appreciate about this book is that it does each of these things very well.

I am a father, and although my children are adults, I still talk to them, so what I read here was enormously revealing, helpful, and encouraging. As I read, a thousand parenting scenes from my life came back to me; some made me thankful, some made me laugh, and some caused me grief. But as I was reliving those scenes, four things came to mind.

1. Our first moment with our daughter Nicole. I will remember this moment forever. Nicole is adopted, and we first set our eyes on her at a gate that had been reserved for us at the Philadelphia airport. She was just four months old, and her escort carried her so that little Nikki was facing us as she approached. We were immediately emotional when we saw her little smiling face, but we fell apart when the escort handed this little human being to us and then faded into the background. In a moment a human life had been handed to us and placed in our care. The inescapable significance of what it means to be a parent hit us harder than it had ever hit us before. God had placed a life in our hands—a totally dependent little person whose life would be largely shaped by what we decided for her, how we acted in relation to her, and what we would say to her.

The one we held in our hands would have her view of herself shaped by us and her knowledge of God formed by us. Her perspective on relationships would come from us, her sense of right and wrong would be sculpted by us, and all of this would be built by thousands and thousands of interactions we would have with her. We felt overwhelmed, unprepared, and unworthy, and because we did, we cried out to God for the grace to represent him well in this little one's life. As I have written elsewhere, we were impressed that few things are more important in life than to be God's tool for the formation of a human soul.[1]

2. *The incredible power of words.* By words God created this amazing cosmos out of nothing. By words God revealed to us the story of redemption and all the explanatory truths attached to it. By words Jesus showed us the heart of the Father and the nature of his kingdom. By words Jesus healed the sick and brought dead people back to life. By words the apostle Paul explained to us what grace looks like and how it operates. By words Satan tempts us to doubt God's wisdom and goodness and to step beyond God's boundaries. Words are powerful.

With words you can bring tears to your child's eyes. With words you can give a hopeless child a reason to continue. With words you can help a lonely and alienated child feel loved and accepted. With words you can light fires of anger in a child's heart. With words you can calm the storm of your troubled child's emotions. With words you can help a spiritually blind child to see God. With words you can stimulate a rebellious child to consider doing

---

1. Paul David Tripp, *Parenting: 14 Gospel Principles That Can Radically Change Your Family* (Wheaton, IL: Crossway, 2016), 21.

what is right. With words you can begin the process of healing a broken relationship. With words you can help a child interpret the past and you can lay out warnings for the future.

Words are powerful. You will speak to your child, and what you say will always produce some kind of harvest in your child's heart and mind.

3. Speaking the truth is not always helpful. This may surprise you as you read it, but this book reminded me of how important it is to understand this concept. Truth can be a wonderful tool of grace or a weapon of destruction. You can say something true to your child, but in a way that is meant to hurt him. You can speak truth to your child in a public setting that unnecessarily embarrasses her. You can use truth to never let your child live beyond past wrongs. Truth is a tool of vengeance or a tool of forgiveness. It is a tool to tear down or to build up. Truth can open up a heart or cause it to be defensive. Few things are more important in your parenting than the way you use the tool of truth.

This is why the Bible calls us to "[speak] the truth in love" (Eph. 4:15) or to only speak words "that give grace to those who hear" (Eph. 4:29). You will know things about your children—things about their personality, their strengths and weakness, their susceptibilities, their past choices, their level of maturity, their spirituality, their best and worst moments. It is nearly impossible to overestimate the importance of the way you use the truth that you know about your children in the thousands and thousands of moment-by-moment, day-by-day encounters that God has planned for you to have with them.

4. The impossibility of what God calls us to do and say as parents. It's simply not possible for people who have sin still living inside of them to do what God has called us to do and speak as God has called us to speak on our own. If we are going to speak as God's tools of wisdom, rescue, and transforming grace in the lives of our children, the thing that must happen again and again is not rescue from our children. No, we must be rescued from us.

We need to humbly admit that the words we say come from what is inside of us, not from who our children are and what they have done. We need the grace to admit that our words as parents reveal how much we still need the moment-by-moment rescue and forgiveness of God's grace. We need the grace to be more concerned about the sin that still lives in us than we are about the sin we see in our children. And we all need to remember that no one gives grace more lovingly and patiently than the parent who confesses how much he needs it himself. And finally, God never calls us to do something without enabling us to do it, and he never sends us somewhere without going with us.

These four thoughts were not only stimulated by this book, but they also form the reason why I think this book is so helpful and encouraging. Bill Smith knows the significance of the parental calling, he knows well the power of words, he understands that speaking truth is not always helpful, and he gets how dependent every parent is on God's ever-flowing bountiful supply of grace. Because of this, I can tell you for sure that this book will change the way you think about the way you talk not only to your child, but also to every other person in your life. But this book did something else to me and I think it will to you too: it made me even more thankful for the person, presence, power, and grace of Jesus.

I joyfully recommend any book that reminds parents of the grace of Jesus, because living with that awareness changes how you act toward and how you speak to your children, and this book does that as well as any parenting book I have read. Read and allow God to use Smith's wise counsel to sharpen you as God's tool of grace in the lives of those he has entrusted to your care.

Paul David Tripp
December 2018

Introduction

It was a difficult conversation, and it wasn't getting better. My son and I squared off in the living room, and you could feel the tension building with each interchange as each person dug in, hardening his position. You could see it in our faces. You could hear it in our voices and in the words we used. The situation wasn't out of control yet, but there was no sign of it moving in a healthy direction either.

Then at one particularly strained moment I was struck by the thought, "Be really careful right now, because what you say next will impact your relationship with him well beyond today." That moment of insight helped reshape what I said. It didn't immediately defuse everything, but you could sense the atmosphere in the room starting to change. We were now working toward a resolution rather than further escalation. Thinking about the future and what I wanted for the two of us in that future affected what I said in the present and helped set us on a different course.

That conversational moment was uniquely charged, but at its essence, it was like any other. The things you choose to say or not to say, along with how you say them, will either invite the people around you to enjoy greater relationship with you or warn them against having anything more to do with you. Every conversation comes with a silent, implied question that asks, "Would you be interested in building an ongoing friendship with me in the future based on how you are experiencing me right now?"

The awareness of that unspoken invitation was profoundly helpful to me in transforming what I was about to say to my son and how I said it, both in that moment and in many conversations since.

That awareness was also profoundly unsettling. I cannot begin to count the number of destructive things I had already said to him over the course of his life or the harmful ways in which I said them. Worse, not only did this insight arrive too late to avoid a checkered past, but it hasn't always had the power to reshape conversations with my son since. My communication failures after that day are also too many to count.

But that doesn't leave me hopeless. Thankfully, what is true of us and our words is also true of God. When he speaks to us, he not only reveals his character and personality, but he also reveals what he's like relationally. Those interactions give us reason to trust him as we learn how he treats us, especially during those times when we make his life more difficult—such as those times when we speak poorly to our children.

As God speaks to us, taking into account our weaknesses, our immaturity, our fearfulness, our arrogance, our ignorance, and even our mistrustfulness, we discover someone who is worth knowing—someone who does not hold our sins against us, but treats us better than we deserve.

When he speaks kindly yet directly to us, he gives us reasons to trust him and in turn to want more of him. His words invite long-term relationship as we (re)experience the gospel through them. And as you hear him talk to you, you learn to speak to your children in similar ways that give them reasons to want to continue their conversation with you despite your many missteps.

Part 1 of this book, "The Vision," explores how your words, like God's, either invite or repel long-term relationship. Relationships are dynamic. Ever changing. Each conversation you have alters the relationship, nudging it in one direction or another. The innumerable conversations you have with your kids are daily opportunities to invite them to enjoy building a satisfying, long-term relationship with you. This kind of relationship models what they could have with the God who longs to communicate with people so much that he gave us the gift of language in the first place.

Part 2, "The Hope," recognizes the sad reality, however, that you haven't always said things that foster positive relationships with your kids. Before you can confidently embrace a good future with them, you need reasons to believe that your past failures do not control that future. You need hope that you have not damaged your relationship with your child so badly that it is beyond repair.

The confidence you need can only come from seeing that God does not leave you to your failures. Instead, he continues relating to you, inserting himself into your life to restore you to being the parent he always intended you to be. He comes to you to show you ways of living righteously, even after you've failed, that are guaranteed to restore your relationship with him and that will invite your child to something far better than the two of you have had.

Parts 3 and 4 explore the skills you need to offer that invitation by using Paul's broad rubric of "speaking the truth in love" (Eph. 4:15) as a guide. Both sections will keep tying what we say to our children back to what we've heard from God. We can communicate gospel-rich content that invites them to gospel-centered relationships—with God and with ourselves—only when we speak out of our own reliance on this same gospel.

Part 3, "The Skill of Encouragement," studies the antidote to conversations that more easily speak truth that is not concerned for the other person—when "truth" leaves out love. If that's a temptation for you, then you want to learn to speak truth that builds your children up rather than tears them down.

Part 4, "The Skill of Honesty," looks at the opposite problem of withholding truth out of fear that the other person won't like it—when "love" leaves out truth. If that's your tendency, then you'll want to learn to speak truth courageously, even if it leads to awkward moments, out of a desire to help your children become strong enough to turn away from things that would hurt them.

Let me say one more thing to encourage you before we get started. You don't have to wait until you and your child are in a relationally healthy place to have conversations grounded in the gospel that hold out hope for a good future with him. The gospel doesn't require a positive starting point. It doesn't even require a neutral one. In fact, it's used to entering into the brokenness of human relationships. It thrives there.

You probably already know that. In your own life, the gospel had to begin at a negative place—God came to you and started talking with you after you'd ruined your relationship with him and dug yourself a hole you couldn't climb out of. He didn't wait to get involved until you and he were on good speaking terms. Instead, he optimistically entered into your life, believing that things between the two of you didn't have to stay the way they were. His involvement alone guarantees that your relationship with him will be better than what it was.

Similarly, despite tainted or even broken relationships with your children, you can learn to engage them conversationally in ways that begin to undo the effects of past brokenness and offer them a better future—a better future with you that gives them a taste of what a future could be like with God.

Part 1

THE VISION

Parenting involves countless interactions
through which you invite potential future peers
to an ongoing relationship
if they should so choose.

1

Parenting Is an Invitation

Parenting doesn't work. It woos.

After I finished talking to a mother's group about parenting, one of the ladies came up to me and said, "I see how I've not been very gracious with my kids, so, if I were more gracious with the things that I say and do, then things would probably work better at my house, right?"

Now I don't think she's unusual, but she missed the point of what I was trying to say. The point of parenting is not that things would work better in our homes—that life would be a little easier and that things would run more smoothly. That's not the goal, but it is what she wanted. And so she was looking for some kind of method that, once mastered, would guarantee certain results if only she invested the right amount of time and effort. She wanted something that works.

Parenting doesn't "work." Parenting requires you to invest time and energy without knowing for sure what the outcome will be. That's true of all relationships, but it's surprising when you realize that you're going to pour yourself into your children, bend your life around them, sacrifice for them, change your world for them, and yet have no guarantee they'll respond well.

Who wants that? I don't. I want some certainty. I want some sense that if I say the right thing and do the right thing, then my kids will respond positively to me, and I'll at least get some of the result I'm looking for. Only, there is no certainty. That's probably not what you want to hear. I know it's not what I want to hear.

You and I are not alone. A father put it this way: "I know it's not right, but I'm more inclined to start conversations if I know there's going to be a payoff. If I know that what I'm about to say is going to work, then I'm all in. But if I don't know, if I'm not sure, then I tend to pull back. I'm hesitant to say anything." He's looking for something that increases his odds of a favorable result. He's looking for a guaranteed return before he invests.

I think he's talking for a lot of us. Parenting, however, is not about figuring out the right thing to do or to say to generate a certain outcome; it's about a person to love. And when you're talking about loving a person, you realize there are no formulas that always work, which means there are no guarantees and no certain return on your investment.

Unfortunately, in my experience as a counselor and pastor (and as a parent!), people want that return. And they want it now. And so they talk with their friends and mentors, read books and go to seminars, open to any strategy that holds out hope that they can get as close to a guaranteed result as possible.

They come with a clearly defined problem—either the child is doing something that the parents need to stop or the child is not doing something that the parents want him to start—then they search for a method that promises to address the problem they see.

But therein lies the trap. When you define parenting as an adult-initiated resolution to a problem created by your child, then you'll think primarily in terms of getting your child back in line. In that case, parenting becomes a negative interaction that's trying to end the domestic tension generated between what you want and what your child is doing.

So how do you avoid the trap? You refuse to let yourself think only in terms of what you should or shouldn't do. You make yourself look past the problem to the person—your child—which gets you to think in relational terms not merely behavioral ones.

You think about what it means to love your children in the moment more than loving what you want from them or even what you want for them. It's only as you see and value them as individuals that you have any hope of developing healthy connections with them. Start then by considering, at their most basic, who are they? What's their most fundamental identity?

First and foremost, they're not yours. They're God's. He made them and takes primary responsibility for them. They come under your care only secondarily and even then, only temporarily.

They are your children—they may even have come from your body—but they are also autonomous beings in their own right. When God made them, he did not consult you. You picked out none of their attributes, their virtues, their talents, their gifts, their weaknesses, their insecurities, or their struggles.

In that sense, they are not mini-me's—smaller versions of you whose reason for existence is to reflect your glory and make you look good. Nor are they a slightly subhuman species that needs to be socialized through the use of clever charts to elicit good behavior until they're old enough to survive on their own. They are images of God, independent of you, yet related to you.

That means they are eternal beings, who, having begun life, will continue living indefinitely. Think about the maturity gap between you and them right now. Regardless of how great it is, it will continue to shrink as time goes by, becoming less significant until it's immaterial. In fact, they will surpass you in many areas, if they haven't already. Look into the future: how important will your twenty-five year head start be when you are both ten thousand years old? As your children grow and mature, by God's design, they and you have the potential to become peers.

Parenting, therefore, means I invest in these fellow human beings, but I am not wrapping my world around them nor am I trying to get them to wrap theirs around me. Instead, parenting is the sum total of interactions between two human beings whereby I regularly invite a slightly younger person to a relationship that increasingly closes the maturity gap between us.

God Invites You—You Invite Your Child

The good news for God's people is that you already know what this kind of relationship is like. Even if you're only just getting to know him, you now see things much more like he does than you did before—the gap has shrunk because you've grown. And it will continue to shrink as your Father in heaven parents you.

The apostle Paul talks about how God's people develop, until collectively we are a body whose maturity in every respect matches its head, who is Christ (Eph. 4:15). In the Psalms, Asaph makes obscure comments about people being gods, hinting that we might be more than meets the eye (Ps. 82:6), while Peter declares outright that by God's power, we can now share in his divine nature (2 Pet. 1:3–4; see also Gal. 2:20; 1 John 3:2).

We don't become God. Nor will we ever be God's equal. But God plans a long-term relationship with us, such that we share in his nature and, while not equal to him, we become a partner suitable to him (Eph. 5:31–32). We grow as he interacts with us in the present, with an eye toward the future. Much of that interaction comes from listening to him speak to us—certainly as we pray and even more clearly in the Scriptures.

He talks, and his words draw you to him in the moment because each time he speaks, he tells you about himself. He tells you what he's like—what he values, what's important to him, and what's not. He tells you where his commitments lie and what he thinks is essential in life.

But his words also tell you what he's like relationally—how he treats people, how he expects relationships to work, the role he plays in others' lives, and the role they play in his. And you learn that he doesn't simply treat you well when you've been good. He treats you well when you've not been good—not holding your sins against you, treating you better than you deserve, and all the time speaking kindly yet directly to you. He talks to you in ways you want to be talked to, giving you reasons to want more of him.

As you think about what he's like as a person and how he relates to people, you realize, "I could like someone like that. If that's the kind of person he is and if that's how he treats people, then I want more of that. I want more of him. I'd like to get to know him better."

That's when you realize that his words do more than simply engage you in the present moment. They carry an implied invitation for the future that asks, "Based on what I just said, do you think I am someone who is worth getting to know? Based on how I just spoke to you, am I someone you'd like to have a long-term relationship with?"

His words give you reason to trust him. You listen to him talk in the Bible to people who are weak, damaged, compromised, or in danger, and you discover that he doesn't take advantage of them. He doesn't crush them. Doesn't push them away. Doesn't hate them. His words don't break relationships. Instead, he uses words to foster greater relationship.

As he speaks, we experience the grace of the gospel and it transforms us, becoming part of us, so that his words become part of us. We then speak to those around us in ways similar to how he's spoken to us.

The same dynamic between you and God is at work between you and your children. Every time the possibility of a conversation comes up, you are communicating exactly the same things to them that God communicates to you: "This is what I am like as a person—this is what I value; this is what's important to me; this is how I think about life; this is how I think about you."

And you're also communicating what you're like relationally: "This is what I'm like in a relationship—this is how I treat people; this is how I interact; these are the kinds of things that I say; this is the way that I say them."

And just like God, you're not only communicating those things about the present moment, but you're also inviting the people around you to something more. Whether you choose to speak or choose not to speak, you're not only telling who you are and what you're like relationally, but you're also asking, "Based on what I just said, do you want less of me or more?"

Here's the kicker: you're always doing that. You can't help it. Our children—who in the normal course of life spend a significant amount of their most formative years with us—hear this embedded invitation very clearly. The things we choose to say or not to say, along with the way that we say them, are either an invitation to, or a warning against, greater relationship.

Parenting then is the privilege of wooing potential future peers—smaller, less developed images of God—inviting them, if they so choose, to vertical and horizontal relationships that could outlast time.

Now do you see why parenting doesn't "work"? It can't. You cannot force your children to love you or want to be with you or work well with you. But you can woo. You can give them an experience of living in God's world that invites them to have more. You can use words to love them, pursue them, train them, and engage them like God uses words with you. In doing so your kids will have the chance to sense his character and nature through you, which will help them decide whether or not they'd like more of you and more of him.

This kind of parenting will leave you tired and desperate because you'll realize how little control you have over your child's heart and how few abilities to reach it. That's a good awareness because it will drive you back to Jesus. And as he meets you in your need, you'll be that much better equipped to invite your kids to that same experience for themselves.

This book is an invitation to experience God's heart with your kids, to experience God parenting you as you parent them.

2

The Invitation Is Embedded in Your Conversations

Have you ever thoughtlessly said something that was unkind, sharp, cutting, nasty, embarrassing, or even cruel, then turned around quickly when someone confronted you and said, "Oh, I didn't mean that"?

Jesus would disagree. He explained once that our words give such a good picture of our hearts, our inner worshiping core, our essential nature, that "on the day of judgment people will give account for every careless word they speak, for by your words you will be justified, and by your words you will be condemned" (Matt. 12:36–37).

Notice that it's not the carefully constructed, well-rehearsed things that come out of our mouths that reflect what is most true of us. It's the careless ones. It's the ones that just slip out without our having to think about them that best reflect our true essence.

They reveal something of us as individuals—what we value, what we wrap our lives around, what we most cherish and will least let go of. The careless, uncensored words show how we understand our God and our place in his universe. They show what we worship. And those same words that lightly trip off our tongues show how our worship affects everyone around us.

That means our words, especially the quick, easy, careless ones, reveal what kind of relationship we will create because they show the place and value that others have in our lives. This place and value doesn't merely affect the present moment, but promises to shape the future as well.

So take a moment and think: what do your kids hear from you? If they regularly experience you as harsh, strict, overbearing, joyless, gloomy, never satisfied, depressed, or needy, then it's because you've told them that you cherish something deep inside—only it's not them. It's something else, and their role in life is to make sure you have that other thing.

Most often that means you've communicated that you expect some form of hassle-free living from them with as few interruptions as possible while they give you the love and respect you feel entitled to by virtue of how much you do for them. If that's their present experience of you, you probably shouldn't be too surprised if they decide they don't want a whole lot to do with you as they get older and have more relational opportunities from which to choose. Why would they? You've given them no good reason to want more of you.

On the other hand, if they experience you as someone who is candid, frank, nurturing, caring, gentle, fun, concerned, engaging, trustworthy, truthful, and wise, they're picking that up because you're speaking out of a set of values that cares for them. You've communicated that you are more interested in their well-being than in your own comfort. And so you are willing to step up and speak in ways that offer them the opportunity to mature into all that God ever intended them to be.

Words that create that second kind of experience also imply that there's more future goodness in a relationship with you. You've given them a reason to stay connected. True, there's no guarantee, but which is more likely: that they'd want to continue a relationship with someone who is cranky and never satisfied or with someone who engages them for their benefit?

When what I most value at the core of my being is my relationship with God and others, then my words will reflect that reality in a way that people can believe. And that reality will be most deeply felt when others are not at their best.

Anyone can say, "I like you" when you're likeable. But when you're not likeable and someone still speaks gently, courageously, to woo you and bring you back, then you see how deeply committed they are to you. You see their heart. And you experience the goodness of their heart in the kind of relationship they create between you, giving you a taste of what you can expect from them in the future. When that happens, you want more of it; you want more of them.

Misplaced Worship Generates Uninviting Relationships

The obvious question then is: "Why would you ever want to speak in a way that would drive people away rather than invite them closer?" And the answer, according to Jesus is: "You can't help it. You always speak out of what you worship. So if you value something more highly than you value God, then you'll engage people out of that value and end up speaking badly."

For instance:

- If you worship accomplishing your goals—if Achievement and Success are your gods—then don't be surprised that you mostly talk to your kids when you need them to work with you to get something done and tend to ignore them otherwise.
- If you worship Efficiency—having a smooth-running life— then don't be surprised that most of what you say to your kids is to correct problems.
- If you worship being Respectable, then most of what you say will be about helping them learn how not to embarrass you.

- If you worship feeling Needed by other people, then don't be surprised that you primarily engage your kids when they're struggling, that you're actually happier when your kids are upset and have a problem that you can drop in and fix, and that you're driven by crisis more than nurturing.

Hate feeling lonely? You'll smother your kids with words. Have to be perfect? You won't be able to admit to them that you were wrong. Have to protect yourself from being hurt? Their apologies will never be enough.

You will speak to them out of what you worship.

I look at that list and see me over and over again. I can't go a single day without saying something stupid or wrong, because my worship gets misplaced every day. That's when I need to know one more time that there is hope for me that doesn't rely on how strong my heart is for God. I need to know how strong his is for me. That means I need to go back and hear him speak to people who struggle to keep their worship focused on him. People just like me.

Listen to him talk to people who are weak, damaged, compromised, or in danger—people like you and me—and you'll see that he doesn't hurt them or take advantage of them, not even when they threaten to break relationship by valuing something more than they value him. Instead, he employs words to build even stronger relationships with them. Let's listen in on his conversations with some of his friends in the next chapter.

3

How Jesus Talks to Estranged Friends

In the opening chapter of the book of Revelation, one of Jesus's disciples, John, seems to be praying. He says he was "in the Spirit on the Lord's day," when Jesus suddenly appeared to him (Rev. 1:10).

And John was terrified. He came face-to-face with the risen Christ, and Jesus was no longer covering up his glory. He was no longer masquerading as a mere mortal. Instead, blinding light was streaming from within him; power was pouring out of him. And John was so overwhelmed that he passed out (Rev. 1:17).

Now John doesn't know it yet, but he is about to hear how this old broken world ends and the new restored one begins. He's about to hear how the Enemy of God and God's people will fight against God and how God will win. The account is going to be couched in epic kinds of scenes—signs in the heavens, angelic hosts warring with demonic spirits, plagues and famine convulsing the world, blood running freely, death and destruction everywhere—until all creation is wiped clean again.

But before that happens, before there's any glimpse into heaven or into the future, this awe-inspiring, terrifying God opens his mouth to talk. And he talks to his people, his bride. He singles out seven churches that existed at the time and talks to them. Listen to how he begins talking to the first one:

> To the angel of the church in Ephesus write: "The words of him who holds the seven stars in his right hand, who walks among the seven golden lampstands.
> "I know your works. . . ." (Rev. 2:1–2)

If you don't know what's coming next, that might not sound all that positive. The risen Christ who is terrifying just to look at, just said, "I know you." The awe-inspiring God who is stronger than death just said, "I know you." You can't hide from him. You can't get away with anything. "I know you *and* I'm going to talk to you about what I know."

I can think of ways he might finish that sentence that wouldn't be positive:

- As an accusation: "I know you . . . and I'm really disappointed in you."
- With mistrust: "I know you . . . and I'm not taking my eyes off you for one second."
- With rejection: "I know you . . . and I want nothing to do with you."

So what comes next is very important because whatever he says next is going to tell you not just what he knows about *you*, but it's going to tell you about *him*. It will tell you what he's feeling right now. It will tell you what he thinks is important. It will tell you things that he likes or doesn't like. It will tell you what kind of person he is. You can't see this God, but when he opens his mouth next, you'll know something about him because he's about to tell you what he thinks about you.

I know your works, your toil and your patient endurance [Whew, okay, this is better than I was hoping for], and how you cannot bear with those who are evil, but have tested those who call themselves apostles and are not, and found them to be false. I know you are enduring patiently and bearing up for my name's sake, and you have not grown weary. (Rev. 2:2–3)

He just said, "I know you, and I'm pleased with you. I know you, and I wanted you to know that I know you and that I am proud of you." God is initiating a conversation, and it's positive. He sees good things and calls you out for them. That's when you learn he's not a God who is cranky and grumpy and unhappy and never pleased. He can be really happy about you. And not only is he happy about you, but when he is, he tells you that he is. He encourages you.

But he also has other things to say as well:

But I have this against you, that you have abandoned the love you had at first. Remember therefore from where you have fallen; repent, and do the works you did at first. If not, I will come to you and remove your lampstand from its place, unless you repent. Yet this you have: you hate the works of the Nicolaitans, which I also hate. (Rev. 2:4–6)

Notice here that God sees the negatives just as clearly as he sees the positives. And he talks about them just as strongly as he talks about the positives. He's really not happy, and yet, he's not losing it. He's not raging or scary. He's clear, but not crushing.

He says what he does in a way that doesn't drive you away. Instead, there's an invitation: "You're not right with me, but you could be. Please change so that we're in step with each other again."

As you keep reading, you realize he's working hard to underline the invitation: "He who has an ear, let him hear what the Spirit says to the churches. To the one who conquers I will grant to eat of the tree of life, which is in the paradise of God" (Rev. 2:7).

He wants them to be right with him so that they can be with him, and so he offers incentives to urge them along.

When we continue reading what Jesus says to the other six churches, we learn even more about the kinds of things he says to his people, because to each church he says, "I know you":

- I know your deeds, both good (Rev. 2:2, 19; 3:8) and bad (Rev. 3:1, 15).
- I know how hard life is for you (Rev. 2:9, 13).
- I know your passion for me or your lack of passion for me (Rev. 2:13; 3:8, 15).

Over and over again: I know you, I know you, I know you, I know you . . . and I talk to you. I talk to you about what I know, and I talk to you to urge you on:

- I talk to you to encourage you (Rev. 2:10, 24–25; 3:4, 10).
- I talk to you to help you see where you're not right (Rev. 2:4, 14–15, 20; 3:17–18).
- I talk to you to warn you of what will happen if you don't change (Rev. 2:5, 16; 3:16).
- I talk to you to remind you that it's worthwhile to know me (Rev. 2:7, 11, 17, 26–28; 3:5, 12, 21).

God is saying very specific things to his people two thousand years ago that address them and their needs of the moment, but he's doing so much more. He's telling you, "This is what my voice sounds like. These are the kinds of things that I say and the kinds of things I don't say. This is what you can expect to hear from me."

It would have been so easy for him to say, "I know you and I . . . ignore you, give you the silent treatment, belittle you, lecture you, berate you, cajole you, beg you, or bribe you." He could have said all that, but he didn't.

Think of who's doing the talking. He's the Lion of Judah who was slain as a Lamb in order to rescue the churches he's been talking to (Rev. 5:5–10), and after all that he's done for them, they're still only half-heartedly pursuing him or substituting other things for him. Why bother talking to them?

Because he loves them: "Those whom I love, I reprove and discipline" (Rev. 3:19). His hope is that by talking to them, they'll turn around and rekindle their friendship with him. Jesus pictures himself as knocking on a door, wanting them to respond, and if they do, he offers to come in and eat with them (Rev. 3:20). To share a meal. To share life. To restore relationship. To deepen friendship. And don't forget: he pursues them for relationship after they had one with him but lost interest in him.

That's a God I can love: one who sees my need and continues to use his words to meet my need. Any other God I couldn't love. A harsh god would not be safe to open my heart to. Nor would an indifferent god. A needy god who put up with whatever I dished out wouldn't be worthy of respect. I could serve and obey any of those gods, but I couldn't love them. And I only know this side of Christ's worth and value because he makes the effort to talk with me about what is pulling me away from him.

When my heart lines up with his—when I care more about my friendship with him and with others than I care about what I can get from others—then my words will sound more like his. Yours will too. You learn to trust God's heart for you based on his words to you when you're not at your best, and your kids learn to trust your heart for them based on your words to them when they're not at theirs.

4

Extended Story: Sacred Space

God's working assumption, after sin ruined this world, is that every conversation with human beings occurs when they're not at their best. As good and enjoyable as you and your children can be, no one is yet as good as God's children will be. You can't expect, then, to have conversations within a perfect family. You can, however, expect your kids to create opportunities that are perfect for communicating the grace you have received as God has perfectly embraced you with your imperfections.

These opportunities don't come with cue cards, however. Most of the time they're disguised as ordinary, everyday interruptions to what you had planned to do or what you had wanted to get out of life. Get used to looking for them. Take advantage of them. They're too good to miss and too fragile to handle roughly. Here's what one looked like in my family.*

We had finished dinner earlier, cleaned and tidied up afterward, resolved all outstanding homework problems, and were settling in for the night. I had retired to my office with a new book, hoping it would be worth reading. Just a normal, ordinary evening with no hint of anything special on the horizon.

One of the kids found me at my desk, however, and asked, "Do you have a minute?"

"Sure," I said and put down my book, hoping they'd be quick. "What's up?"

"About two or three years ago I saw a ten-dollar bill on the table at your place and thought it would be a great way for me to get rich, so I took it. And you knew I did because you saw it on my bedside table later. But I told you I didn't know how it got there and that one of the cats must have brought it up from the dining room. Do you remember that?"

"Yeah," I said, fully engaged now, "I do." It had been an awful couple of months. We were pretty sure we knew what had happened, but this precious child had stubbornly refused to admit it. They had even tried to give me the ten dollars back, but had stuck to their story about a thieving house pet. I hadn't taken the money because the issue was never about the money; it was about their heart that they were holding back from the rest of us.

"Well," they continued, opening their wallet, "it was wrong, and I was wondering what I should do. Do you want the money back?"

This is sacred space—the presence of God, unlooked for, unannounced, invading my office. What an amazing moment to be part of. A true prodigal, interested more in their parent's possessions than in a relationship with him, was now interested in coming home. And yet, as is the nature of prodigality, they were hoping to square accounts unilaterally on their own terms.

I thought maybe a subtle question would help. "Wow. Thank you for saying that. Um . . . are you suggesting that you can pay me back for what you did?"

"Yes," came the quick, confident reply.

Okay, maybe I was too subtle. I smiled and said, "So, you think you can pay me back for how worried I was that you were hardening your heart, that you were pulling away from us? You can pay me back for the suspicions we had over the next several months when other money went missing? You can somehow make up for my concern that you were practicing greed and deception as a way of life?"

More sobered now, they looked down and said, "No. I can't."

"So what do you need to do?"

"Ask Jesus to forgive me?"

"Yes!" I said, "And he will. He promises that when you confess your sins, he will forgive you. And I will too. I am really proud of you for coming to me and telling me. This helps me trust you. When you tell me things I couldn't know about you, then I know I can trust our relationship because it means more to you than hiding the embarrassing things that you did. Thank you."

I paused then said, "I am curious, though. Why bring this up now?"

"I don't know. It's something that just popped into my mind, and I knew I needed to say something to you."

I said, "That's the Spirit of God at work in your life, bringing things up that you need to deal with. There have been times in my life, seasons, when God has reminded me of things I did wrong that I needed to get right with other people. Why don't you go spend some time with him and see if there's anything else he wants to show you?"

The little person went away to pray, and I marveled at the goodness of a God who keeps track of things for years that have harmed relationships, not to condemn, but to bring about restoration. He patiently waits for the time that best fits into his plan of making both you and your child more like Jesus.

Get as much out of those moments as you can. Don't waste all the thoughtful care and energy he's pouring into them. Instead, just briefly pause before turning back to your book or whatever else you were doing, and think about how you can work alongside what he's doing. For me that meant I wanted not only to affirm my child for their courage, but to try giving them a sense of God's heart as well, so when they came back from praying I asked, "Do you remember the story of the prodigal son?"

"Yeah."

"How does it end?"

"When the kid comes home, the dad throws a big party for him."
"That's right," I said, "because he's so glad to have his child
back." My child smiled. "That's a picture of how God rejoices
when someone turns away from sin. And right now that's how
God feels about you. And so do I. This is a good moment."
It got better. They then told me they needed to go ask Mommy's forgiveness for some other things and walked off like it was
a perfectly normal thing to do. And it is.

That's what it looks like when God breaks into our small, carefully organized, mundane worlds to offer us the chance to have
conversations with our kids like he has with us. It is so much more
wonderful than any book or other distraction could be. It is worth
any interruption. And it is so delicate.

You have to be ready for it. Ready to drop everything else to
prize it. You have to take seriously the warning label—Handle
with Care—that comes with it because people are even more vulnerable than usual. You have to work hard, gently challenging
them, drawing them out, affirming them, interpreting what's happening, guiding their next steps, and celebrating with them. It
would be exhausting if it weren't so exhilarating. And it's possible
only because he continues to work through imperfect people in
imperfect settings in order to perfect both.

*A big thank-you goes to my children for giving me permission to tell their stories in this
book and for their help in recollecting the details.

5

You Talk with No Guarantee

Now you might be thinking, "Okay, this sounds good when everything works out well. But what about when it doesn't? What then? I'm just supposed to keep inviting, keep talking, without knowing if I'm actually getting through to my kids? That's not fair. It's not like God does that—wondering if his words are making a difference or if he's just wasting his breath—does he? I mean, he already knows the future, chooses his children, and changes their hearts, so he's never in danger of watching his words get squandered, right?"

Actually, God's situation is worse than yours precisely because he knows the future. He has to decide whether to say things or not say things, even when he already knows that he'll be dismissed as irrelevant. If that were my reality, then I wouldn't bother talking at all with anyone whom I knew was going to reject me. The fact that he engages those people and initiates conversations with them is pure kindness on his part; it's kindness that's in line with his character.

God makes his rain fall on the righteous and the unrighteous alike (Matt. 5:45). He reaches out over long periods of time to people who despise him (Isa. 65:1–5) and reveals himself to his creatures even if they won't take him up on his invitation to know him (Ps. 19:1–4; Rom. 1:20). God bases his decision to communicate on something other than the certainty that he'll be received.

Think of his interaction with Adam's son, Cain. God first comes to him and warns him that sin is about to master him (Gen. 4:6–7). That's nothing but pure grace on God's part. Cain pointedly ignores him by killing his brother. In response, God again comes to him (grace again) and starts another conversation (more grace) by asking a question (grace upon grace!) (Gen. 4:9). God did not withhold his words even though in his omniscience he knew that he'd be ignored. Why say anything then? Because Cain needed to hear those words at that moment of his life, even though he would reject them.

Or consider Jonah. Among other things, the book of Jonah is a story of God relentlessly engaging a man who keeps turning away from him. You really see God's pursuit in the last chapter, where he repeatedly invites Jonah to extend the same kind of grace to others that he himself has received (Jonah 4:4, 9–11). The story ends ambiguously, however, as God's final question hangs in the air unanswered. Having no idea what Jonah did next invites you to write yourself into the story by considering how you would respond to God's question. It also helps you realize that invitations to conversations, even when they come from one's Maker, are not always accepted.

The story of Jesus's interaction with Nicodemus (John 3:1–21) ends with a similar ambiguity. Does Nicodemus become born again? There are hints in the rest of the book that sure sound like he did (John 7:45–52; 19:38–42). On the other hand, John never uses his special code word for saving faith in conjunction with Nicodemus; he never says Nicodemus "believed." The case is left open, on purpose. It forces you to ask yourself, "Am I born again? Do I believe?" but it also indicates that Jesus was willing to talk with Nicodemus in a way that made sense to the man, while leaving open the potential that Nicodemus might reject what he said.

That's why the story of the prodigal son ends as it does. Clearly the Father is offering as much grace to the older brother as to the younger, but the offer is different. The father doesn't wait for this son to come to him; rather, he leaves the party he gave for the younger son to pursue his older, straying one. And when he finds him he talks to him—not with a harsh rebuke or lecture, but with a gracious, winsome invitation—an invitation to restore relationship with his younger brother and with himself (Luke 15:31–32).

Then abruptly, the story ends. Full stop. You're left wondering, "Wait, what happened? Did the older son repent, jolly up, and go in with his dad? Or did he remain outside, sullen and estranged?" You don't know. You're not told. And Jesus doesn't satisfy your curiosity, because the story itself is an invitation—an offer of a conversation—to the hard-hearted, older-brother-Pharisees from a gracious God who would gladly give them all that he has, knowing that they might very well reject his words outright.

When you're thinking about loving a person, you realize there are no guarantees. There's no certain return on your investment. God doesn't act like there is. He reaches out patiently, repeatedly to his children without telling you how they respond precisely because real love has no guaranteed outcome. But it tries anyway.

Why does it do so?

First, reaching out is what people need. What do your kids need when they're in trouble, overwhelmed, making foolish decisions, needing guidance, feeling alone, pulling away, stuck in their stubbornness? They need someone who cares enough about them to reach into their world, despite the risk of rejection, and speak in such a way to offer them what they need.

Second, love starts conversations without knowing where they'll end up because it's one way we verbally express the reality that it is better to give than to receive (Acts 20:35). If the only time I'll talk to my kids is when I'm certain that I can shape an outcome I want, then I'm not really focused on them and their best interests. Instead, I'm caught up in my agenda and no longer considering my child as someone whose thoughts, opinion, desires, and interests are as important as my own.

Third, love initiates conversations because the potential of a restored relationship is worth far more than its guaranteed absence. When your kids are difficult, it is so much easier to lecture, command, dictate, say as little as possible, shame, or even say nothing at all than it is to invite them to a conversation. In other words, when they are unlovely, it's easy not to love them in return.

But consider: when you refuse to issue an invitation, you are giving your kids no reason to attempt rebuilding their relationship with you. Perhaps they will anyway, but at best it will be despite you. At worst, you'll have given them a disincentive, a reason to believe, "Well, obviously my folks don't care enough to sit down and talk with me so I must not matter to them very much."

Next time you are tempted not to engage your child, try asking yourself, "In six months, which will I regret more: having tried and been rejected, or not having tried and been part of the rejecting?"

Last, you love your kids by entering uncertain conversations with them because God shares himself more deeply with those who experience getting rejected, as he has (1 Pet. 4:14).

My family went away for our annual vacation one year, and I had really gone over the top preparing for it. I thought about it in advance—pulled together books I thought each person would like, games to play, food to eat, movies to watch—because I wanted it to be a real break for everyone.

And it was a disaster. There was constant complaining, fighting, bickering, and squabbling. Nothing was ever good enough. Someone was regularly upset, and somehow I seemed to end up in the middle of it, taking the brunt of their unhappiness. I tried my best to talk with people to help get them on board with loving each other, and nothing I did worked.

After several days of this, I turned to an Old Testament passage that pictures God's relationship with his people. It's about a shepherd who took over a flock of sheep that had been mistreated. He was really excited and worked hard to care for them, but the end result of all his efforts was that "the flock detested me, and I grew weary of them" (Zech. 11:8 NIV).

I sat back and thought, "Wow, that's God's experience of his people—they detested him. And having tried to shepherd my family, that's what I'm experiencing. I'm sharing something similar with him and getting a feeling for some of his heart this week."

That was a good moment—a comforting moment of identification with my God. But then as I sat there, I realized, "Oh, wait. I'm also part of the flock that hated him . . . and yet, he doesn't hate me. He still loves me even though I've detested him and his attempts at parenting me."

It became an opportunity to see more of God and his heart, and even better, to experience his kindness to me at a deeper level. And it was that experience that rejuvenated my desire to go back to my family and to try reaching out to them again. God used what looked like a loss of relationship with them to produce greater connections, first with him and then afterward, with them.

God pours out his kindness by speaking the words people need to hear even when he knows they will reject him. He now invites you to join him by giving yourself to conversations with others— especially your children—with that same exhausting, profligate abandon that's more interested in love than it is in guarantees.

6

You Speak out of the Grace You've Already Heard

Let me give you a negative picture that shows what you're not trying to do when you talk to someone. God embeds this picture in the book of Proverbs in a long, colorful list of what a foolish person is like (Prov. 26:1–12). Several of the verses characterize the worthlessness and danger of communicating with a fool (vv. 4–7), but verse 9 is especially vivid:

> Like a thornbush in a drunkard's hand
> is a proverb in the mouth of a fool. (NIV)

Can you see the fool? This person staggering around, flailing wildly with a branch covered with spikes? The only reasonable response when you see him coming is to warn others, "Look out! Get away from him!"

That's what it's like to converse with fools. They are going to hurt you. There's no intentionality, but simple, uncontrollable blundering that's so damaging that even if they attempt to speak God's wisdom, it has the same effect as being violently raked by thorns.

God never comes at you waving a thornbush of words. If he did, you'd back way off—and you should. Instead, he sounds different. And for us humans it's surprising. As Jesus talked, God's Word made flesh, people "marveled at the gracious words that were coming from his mouth" (Luke 4:22).

The predominant thing people heard from Jesus was not irritation, condescension, frustration, manipulation, hostility, bullying, threats, complaints, whining, or bitterness. They heard gracious words. His words announced that God had come to rescue them, not to crush them (Luke 4:16–21). Not everyone received those words (4:22–30), but it was clear nonetheless that what Jesus spoke was gracious. That's what should amaze people about the way you sound.

Read the Scriptures looking for gracious words from God, and you start to see them everywhere. For instance, you'll hear a God who tells you the following:

- he promises to deliver you from evil (Gen. 3:15);
- he initiated rescuing you (Deut. 5:6);
- you are precious in his eyes (Isa. 43:4);
- he has great plans for you (Jer. 29:11);
- he wants you to be his friend (John 15:15);
- he encourages you (Rom. 15:5);
- he will never give up on you (Phil. 1:6);
- he will not overlook how you've loved him by helping his people (Heb. 6:10); and
- he will wipe away every tear from your eyes (Rev. 7:17).

Look, and you will find words that convince you he really is a God of all grace (1 Pet. 5:10).

Why is this important for you and how you communicate to others? Because the words you use always reflect what you yourself have known. It's as you live in a gracious relationship with God that you have a sense of what grace sounds like and, therefore, you have a sense of what to say to others.

Conversely, if you don't have a regular experience of God speaking graciously to you, then you won't be able to give grace to the people around you. That doesn't mean you won't speak to them, but it means that you'll default to speaking differently out of a different experience—a nongracious one.

Did the people you grew up with have a phrase they used that you hated and swore to yourself, "When I have kids of my own, I will never say that to them"? Maybe something like, "I'm going to tan your hide" or "I'm going to bang your heads together." Some kind of ugly threat that was all about misused power and abuse of authority that created an indelible picture in your mind. Something you absolutely hated.

Now, fast-forward to one of those weeks where the kids have been at each other for days and won't leave each other alone. You're trying to get something done, but their wrangling breaks into your concentration, keeping you from what you wanted to do. You push yourself away from email again, stop trying to sort out the latest credit card statement, put down your hammer for the ninth time in two hours, and that phrase is right on the tip of your tongue. It feels like it's all you can do to choke it back and not let it strike out.

Why? Because you speak out of your experience. You've been taught through the years, "This is what is appropriate to say in moments like these. Say something that will: threaten, whine, argue, debate, insult, complain, or lash out. Say it because it will get you what you want. Say it because it sounds normal under these circumstances." The problem is, that phrase doesn't sound a bit like God.

Your Words Are Powerful Because They're Spoken by God's Image

In the opening chapters of Genesis, God makes images of himself—representatives of himself on earth—people who will visibly express what he himself is like. They are to engage all of creation in the same way that he does, providing a picture of the invisible God to the rest of the watching universe (Rom. 1:18). These images are to act like God acts and think like God thinks, with the same attitudes and longings that God has. Everything about them is to declare, "Here's what God is like!" including when they talk with each other.

That means when you speak or act, you do so as far more than Robert or Mary or Kim or José—one tiny, often overlooked individual, lost among billions of others. Rather, you speak and act as God's representative. Every time you engage others, you are hooked up to a megaphone that amplifies what you do through the cosmos, giving people an experience of how God himself would respond if he were here.

That's why what you do is so powerful. Did you ever compliment someone or encourage him and he got all silly because you touched something in him way deep down? Have you ever urged someone on and watched him try harder? Have you ever extended kindness to someone and watched him melt? In part, they reacted that way because what you did spoke more loudly than you ever intended. What you did communicated something positive of God and his perspective to his other images.

Your actions and interactions come with power because of who God made you to be, but sadly, they can also come with powerful harm because Adam and Eve chose to reject their unique status as God's representatives. They stopped listening to him when they elevated the serpent's words over his. No longer were God's ways and values their greatest treasure. Now they had a new treasure that brought new values, new commitments, new life goals such that everything about them realigned with their new treasure, including the way they interacted with each other.

Jesus says it like this in Luke 6:45: "The good person out of the good treasure of his heart produces good, and the evil person out of his evil treasure produces evil, for out of the abundance of the heart his mouth speaks." Each time you open your mouth to speak or move your hands to act, you are drawing on what you've stored up inside and you are expressing what is inside of you.

Adam and Eve no longer acted on God's behalf because they had absorbed Satan's voice into their very being. You hear the difference immediately as they used words to shift blame away from themselves onto everyone else around them. They didn't entirely lose the power that God created his images to have, but they twisted it. Instead of using their power to build up and strengthen each other, they tried to crush and use each other.

Have you ever had someone insult you or criticize you or take something from you that was important to you and that experience went way down deep into your core—so far down that you just couldn't get past it? That's not simply because you're "sensitive." Those words and actions hurt because they came from someone who was designed to represent God's own heart and mind to you. Those actions weren't God's, but they seem to come from him because his image is speaking them.

And so those words and actions declare, "Here's what your Maker and Creator thinks of you. He thinks you're no good. He thinks you never have been and never will be. He thinks you're a loser. He despises you and thinks you're not worth the trouble." That person took the power of God, but used it to declare the voice of the serpent because that person had stored up his values.

In other words, there are no ordinary, everyday conversations. Each time you engage others you are adding your voice to an ongoing cosmic struggle that started long before humans entered the conflict—you are choosing to add a perspective, a viewpoint, a flavor either of what it's like to live with the Great Creator or what it's like to be around the Deceiver.

You speak out of what you know and as you do, you contribute to what other people know. Your experience has shaped the content of what you say and how you handle yourself, which in turn now gives other people an experience that shapes the content of what they say and how they'll live. Your words are more important than you can possibly begin to imagine.

7

Extended Story:
"Get in the Van"

After church one Sunday my family was getting ready to visit with Mom-mom and Pop-pop for Easter dinner. When we need to coordinate our schedules, I try to give us plenty of advance notice so that everyone can plan their lives accordingly. So as we were getting ready to leave, I said to the kids, "Make sure you've got all your stuff together, because we're going to go in about ten minutes."

Ten minutes later, as I was about to walk out the door, I called out, "Okay, everybody, get in the van." Immediately, they all jumped up from what they were doing and raced in every direction possible, except toward the van. This one ran to the bathroom. Another went to collect books and toys for the trip. Someone else needed their shoes. And I was left standing in the middle of the living room, alone, with nobody getting in the van.

Now, what are my options in that moment? Option 1: come down hard on people. I could stand there and yell: "I said, 'Get in the van' and I mean *now*!" Or I could follow people around, badgering and nagging them: "What do you think you're doing? I know you heard me. What's wrong with you? Why don't you ever listen?" Or I might vent a little more strongly: "Your problem is you never listen because you don't care about anyone else except yourself." The list goes on of all the heavy-handed tactics I have tried in the past and that I could have used again.

What might happen if I went down that road (again)? Well, first of all, it would probably work. They'd get in the van—if for no other reason than to escape me. But there'd also be silence. There might be fear. Certainly they would resent being mistreated. There would be no relationship. They'd hate the way I lead the family, and I'd teach them that authority is overbearing.

There's something much worse, however: I would communicate a false gospel. Because I engage them as God's representative, I would teach my family, "This is the Jesus I know. Whenever I mess up, he's harsh. He's abusive and crushing. He can't stand it when I do something wrong because it upsets his agenda. Then, because he didn't get what he wanted, he lashes out at me and won't let up until he's beaten me back into place. You can expect him to do the same with you too."

That's Option 1. Option 2 is just as bad. I could do nothing as I watch everyone scatter until they slowly trickle out to the van in their own good time.

This time the dialogue would be more internal, but just as poisonous as I whine to myself, "No one ever listens to me. I do all the work around here and provide for everyone else, trying to get things ready and make things nice, but they don't care. I don't know why I even bother. The worst is, there's nothing I can do about it except put up with it till they grow up and move out. Guess I'll go sit in the van by myself and hope they don't make me wait too long."

This popular option results in relationships that are just as badly broken as the first, and it also paints an equally distorted picture of God. It communicates, "Jesus pulls away in self-pity whenever you hurt him. He doesn't like it when you ignore him, but he has no real power or plan to help you, so he distances himself from you. He figures he has to guard his own heart since he has to put up with you being hopelessly broken. So go ahead, do whatever you like, whenever you like, but just realize, you're on your own."

Option 1 and Option 2 sound nothing like God. When God speaks, it is always for the purpose of reconciling you to himself—of bringing you back together with him when you've introduced a gap. He always intends his words with his children to restore relationship with himself. And when that's been your experience, you long to pass it on to others.

That's what happened in my living room. It would have been so easy to harangue my family or withdraw bitterly from them. But by God's grace I chose a different option—one that was harder, but better—one that required me to step up and plead with my family to recognize that when I talk, I do so for their good and that they need to get on board with that reality for their sake.

Why did I do that? It's not because I'm a wonderful guy. I have plenty of spectacular failures, as my family well knows. I've exploded angrily or pulled away in self-pity. I'm not a wonderful guy, but I have a wonderful God—a God who didn't reject Adam and Eve when they rejected him and who hasn't rejected me either.

That means I wasn't completely alone in the living room that afternoon. I have a God who doesn't treat me the way I'm tempted to treat my family. I have a God who hasn't abandoned me or driven me away from him. He was there with me and still not treating me badly.

Therefore, regardless of what my family did next, I would lose nothing by trying to respond to them with grace. Even if everything went horribly wrong with my family from that moment forward, my God would still treat me well.

So I stepped into one of my little people's pathway, held my palm up and said, "No. Stop. What are you doing?"

"Going to brush my hair," they said with an edge.

"I told you earlier that we were leaving soon. Why didn't you get ready then?"

"I was reading a book," they said defensively.

"So . . . you were thinking about what you wanted to do or what I asked you to do?"

A little softer this time: "What I wanted to do."

"When I said, 'Get in the van,' I was thinking about what would be good for our whole family, the five of us, and for our grandparents. I was thinking about seven people. How many were you thinking about?"

"One," came the much softer admission.

"Honey," I said, "I love you . . . and that means you can't live your life this small all the time, wrapped up in yourself like you're the only person here. Get in the van."

What did I do? I used the voice God has given me to speak in such a way that I could quietly invite a little person to repent and realign with Jesus and realign with the rest of us. What happened next was amazing. That person actually asked if we could pray as we were driving and led the rest of us in confessing to God and to each other how we had been so self-absorbed. Their change of heart rippled through the rest of the van.

Afterward, we spent the rest of the ride engaged in each other's lives, talking and playing road-sign games together. And that outward movement toward others continued after the ride was over and influenced the way we engaged their grandparents.

I need to speak in ways that represent the Creator's heart to the people around me. And I need to hear his heart from others when they speak into my life.

I need my wife Sally to step into my world when I'm frazzled by things at home and say to me, "I think you need to take a walk to get yourself right with the Lord so that you can live more patiently with us."

I need my daughter, when she sees "the look" of frustration steal across my face to step up and caution, "Easy, Dad."

I need my colleague to prop herself up on my office doorframe and say, "You don't need me to tell you that your lifestyle isn't healthy right now, do you?"

I need people to speak to me from the depths of grace that they have experienced from Jesus. He has put them in my life as his representatives so that I draw closer to Christ and closer to them.

You have that same calling with the people around you. The calling is to drink deeply of his grace and kindness to you and then gently, confidently, talk to your family and friends out of that grace. Talk to them so that they long to realign their lives with him and then reestablish relationship with you.

8

Your Kids Need You to Talk to Them . . . a Lot

Speaking to your children is a high-risk, high-reward activity. You have the privilege of making the invisible God visible—no higher honor!—and yet you might just as easily paint a picture of him that's more demonic than divine.

"In that case, maybe it's better if I say as little as possible. You know, reduce the risk so that my kids are better off." That kind of logic holds a certain appeal. You can't cause problems if you're not involved, right? Not exactly. As tempting as that option is, it creates a different problem by running counter to God's original plan. He has always intended humans to grow and develop through conversations.

Consider the garden of Eden before it was ruined. Humanity was flawless and faultless, but also ignorant. Adam and Eve didn't know critical things about themselves—that they were made in God's image and were to find meaning and purpose by relating to him as they filled and cared for the earth like God does. They learned those things only when something happened that was simultaneously miraculous and mundane: God spoke to them.

He talked to them, providing them with information they didn't have and could not obtain in any other way. Their ignorance was neither sin-tinged nor the result of evil. It was an immaturity appropriate to their life experience and was removed only by an older, wiser, more experienced person entering into their world with words to help them mature. Perfectly sinless, they were still ignorant and needed to be taught.

If those kinds of conversations were necessary before the blindness and willfulness of sin, can you see how much more necessary they are afterward?

God can. That's why one of the ways we image him is by speaking to others, especially to our children, like he talks with us.

After giving the Ten Commandments to the Israelites— again, God talking to his people, imparting wisdom and knowledge that they could not have if he didn't communicate with them—he told them:

> You shall teach them to your children, talking of them when you are sitting in your house, and when you are walking by the way, and when you lie down, and when you rise. You shall write them on the doorposts of your house and on your gates, that your days and the days of your children may be multiplied in the land that the LORD swore to your fathers to give them, as long as the heavens are above the earth. (Deut. 11:19–21)

Teach and talk everywhere. Verbally communicate not simply what God says, but how his words intersect with daily life as you're home or on the road, as you're sitting, walking, lying down, or getting up. Fill your children's world with God's words so that they develop a sense of who he is, who they are in relation to him, and how they must live in his world.

Your Kids Mature through Conversations

In a perfect universe, God's conversations with Adam and Eve were necessary so that humanity could find their place in his world. After sin ruined everything, such conversations remain foundational. Sin, however, complicates matters. We don't always communicate well with our children, and our children are not always prepared to embrace the process that God designed to serve them best.

One afternoon my elementary-aged son, without a moment's hesitation, shot back at me, "I'm already doing that." I had just tried to offer him a better way to respond to his brother, but he wasn't having it. His response to me came after a weekend of verbal tennis: every time I tried to tell him something about life, he immediately volleyed the ball back with a reason for why he didn't need to hear what I was saying.

So I said, "Wait a minute. Just now there was a conversation that took place inside your head that went something like this: 'Wow! My dad just interrupted what he was doing to speak into my life because he thought there was something I needed to hear, and I am so excited to hear it that I'm going to put all other thoughts out of my head so that I can concentrate on his words. Even if there's only 5 percent of what he says that I don't know, I want to drink it in.' That's what you were thinking just now, right?"

"No," he frowned as he sensed where this was going.

Switching subjects abruptly I asked him, "How long do kittens stay with their moms?"

He shrugged and said, "I don't know, two to three months?"

"Close enough," I thought, so I said, "Okay, but you're here with me and Mom a whole lot longer. Why is that?"

He looked down at the floor and said softly, "Because God thinks I have things to learn."

I nodded my agreement and added, "But you don't want to be here. You're interacting with us assuming you have nothing to learn from us. Each time you do that, you're telling me, 'Dad, I really shouldn't be here right now. I should be out on my own.' You've forgotten why you're here."

Even when he forgets, I have to remember. By God's intent, we enter life knowing nothing, then are slowly brought to understand our world and our place within it through the very ordinary medium of people talking to us. With their help, over time, we mature into contributing, responsible members of society who in turn can support and nurture others. Oddly enough God entrusts our development to people who once were more ignorant than they are now, which in my son's case means me for the foreseeable future.

That process is so commonplace that it is often used to drive the narrative arc of popular literature. A novice—the children of Narnia, the Hobbits of Middle Earth, Harry Potter, Bella the vampire—is plunged into a world that is so unfamiliar that she finds herself floundering in it, not knowing how to respond. Dangers lurk, and her future happiness hangs in the balance with each decision. Then slowly she learns how to navigate and master her new experience because other people talk to her.

They tell her stories that give the world depth and feeling. They instruct her. They correct her. They give her new lenses through which she can see the world and herself more clearly while catching a glimpse of what she and the future might be. She grows impassioned and tries living out what she's been taught. She grows up into more than she ever hoped she could be, all through the ordinariness of talk.

Such coming-of-age stories touch us in part by drawing on the way God has structured his world. We see ourselves in them. We develop our understandings of the world and our place in it by learning from those who already know its ins and outs. At birth we are all novices encountering an alien world that we learn piecemeal, one conversation at a time.

We Never Outgrow Our Need for Transformational Conversations

The book of Proverbs is dedicated to this notion that living well within God's world requires conversation. It takes the form of a father personally addressing his son, passionately pleading with him to gain wisdom and understanding (Prov. 1:8–9). If the son listens, then the father promises that he will escape being a fool and won't ruin his life (1:32–33). That transformation from fool to wise man takes place as one person talks to another about who God is and how he affects all of life.

As you read, however, you realize this isn't simply a book for children, despite addressing "my son" multiple times, because a wise person develops a taste for transforming conversations that continue his entire lifetime. He surrounds himself with a steady rhythmic beat of God-oriented conversations. He welcomes people who will talk to him about himself and about his life and how every part of life relates to God (e.g., Prov. 1:5; 12:5; 15:22).

More than that, he commits himself not simply to hearing from others, but to joining the discussion, speaking to others who want to hear so that their lives will be enriched (e.g., Prov. 12:18; 15:7; 16:23). The book of Proverbs pictures the person who grows wise as someone who swims in a sea of words without drowning.

It's worth noting that even after Jesus pours out his Holy Spirit on his people, he remains committed to maturing his people, in part, through their conversations with each other (e.g., Rom. 15:14; Eph. 5:18–20; Col. 3:16; 1 Thess. 5:14; 2 Tim. 2:2, 24–26; 4:2; Titus 1:9; Heb. 3:13). He expects you to participate in an ongoing, never-ending conversation with his people that links Christ and faith in him to life, because every one of God's people shares in his ministry of words (1 Pet. 4:10–11).

If you reflect just a little on Jesus's life, you realize it's hardly surprising that the church is to have continuous conversations. After all, he talked constantly. He did many good works, but much of his life was devoted to speaking—formal teaching, small group discussions, one-on-one conversations, or just talking with his friends. He was not a man of few words.

And since he unites you to himself and pours his Spirit into you, it only makes sense that you will learn to speak like he does.

He makes godly conversations possible, and he expects you to give yourself to them because the people around you—your children—need them.

In other words, the dynamic set in motion by hearing and then responding to the message of the cross preached is still in motion. We enter into God's family through words, and we grow up in his family through words. We come to understand him, ourselves, others, and our world—and how we fit with him and with others in his world—all through tirelessly conversing with each other.

9

Extended Story: Nanny's Funeral

It was a good death. My grandmother's eyesight had been failing for the past decade till she was nearly blind, and she'd spent the last year confined to a wheelchair in the nursing home. She had been more than ready for her homecoming for quite a while. It was a good death. But it was death. How to break the news to my children?*

We don't do death well in the United States. We hardly acknowledge its existence. Whole industries, from plastic-wrapped, prepackaged meat to hospice care, are dedicated to keeping death's ugly reality safely quarantined in specialized, off-limits locations. We hardly bring death's presence into our conversations, preferring to pretend it's a rare anomaly. Mercifully, Scripture is more in tune with the realities of life than our present culture.

So after dinner I told the kids that Nanny had died that morning and that her funeral would be held a few days later. Immediately, my youngest, Danny, wanted to know if all of us had to go.

Danny really doesn't like death. We were not allowed to talk about our former pet cat who had died three years earlier because of how sad he still felt thinking about her. You could already see him backing quickly away from Nanny's funeral.

Thankfully, I had taken some time earlier in the day to think about how to talk to the kids. In response to Danny's question and to give Cass and Tim a way to process their loss, I turned to a passage in Ecclesiastes 7:2–4 we hadn't discussed before and began reading: "It is better to go to a funeral than to a party" (NCV). Based on the puzzled looks around the table, no one thought that made any sense. I kept reading: "We all must die, and everyone living should think about this. . . . A wise person thinks about death, but a fool thinks only . . ."

"About having fun," Danny jumped in to complete the thought as I paused slightly to let them absorb what we were reading.

Smiling, I said, "That's right! About having fun. 'A wise person thinks about death, but a fool thinks only about having a good time.'"

Another pause, then I asked, "Why is it better to think about death than to have fun? That sounds kind of weird, doesn't it?"

"Yeah." They nodded with thoughtful frowns.

So I asked, "What happens after you die?"

"You go to heaven or hell."

"Okay, but what's so special about going to heaven?"

Timmy said, "Because that's where Jesus is."

"Right. When you die you go to be where Jesus is or you go . . ."

". . . where Jesus isn't," they finished.

"And how long will you be with Jesus or not with Jesus?"

"Forever," they answered.

"Twenty-seven billion years?" I asked.

"Longer," came the chorus from all three.

"Fifty-seven trillion years?"

"Longer," again in unison, but a bit louder.

"So if this life is three-eighths of an inch long," I said, pinching the air with my thumb and forefinger so that there was a tiny gap between them, "and the next life is like from here to the sun—which is about 93 million miles—then which line is it wiser to spend time thinking about? The three-eighths-inch line or the ninety-three-million-mile line?"

"The ninety-three-million-mile line," they agreed.

"That's what I'm going to do next Tuesday. I'm going to go to the funeral and think about the ninety-three-million-mile line. And I think you should go too. You'll be sad and you'll cry—I'm going to cry. Lots. But I'm going to spend time thinking about who I want to be with for ninety-three million miles and what difference that makes in my three-eighths-inch life now."

I continued, "You don't have to go, but I think it will give you a chance to be wise people and think about how this life is just the beginning—the doorway—to the next life and about who you want to be with for the ninety-three-million-mile life."

Everyone decided to go, and a few days later we set out for the funeral. On the way we prayed as a family for our drive, for time with our extended family, and for the uncertainty of the funeral itself. Among other things, Timmy asked Jesus, "Please help me think about the ninety-three-million-mile life this morning and not just this short three-eighths-inch one."

It's a good thing for your kids to learn how to think about hard things. But they can't do it without you. God speaks in such a way to give you a vocabulary to use and a framework that puts even difficult things like death into perspective—a perspective that you and your kids can embrace because his way of thinking makes so much sense. Your voice is essential in calling them to embrace his.

---

*This story originally appeared in my book *Grace through the Ages* (Ambler, PA: Tillett-Consulting, 2012).

Part 2

THE HOPE

Jesus continues to use his mouth
to speak on your behalf
regardless of how badly you've used yours.

10

Sometimes You Don't Want to Talk

Your kids need you to enter their lives intentionally and talk to them about who God is and how he engages his world if they're going to have a chance of seeing him correctly and growing up well in his world. By God's design those opportunities crop up every day, and yet many people back away from them for a variety of reasons. Here's a short list, some of which are probably familiar to you.

You tend not to initiate conversations when you feel:

- *Tired* from a long day.
- *Clumsy* because you never seem to know what to say.
- *Intimidated* by the topic.
- *Consumed* with things that have to get done.
- *Impotent* to solve problems or make them go away.
- *Preoccupied* by something else that you find more interesting.
- *Criticized* whenever you don't say what someone else wants to hear.
- *Scared* that others will shut down if they think you're being nosy.

- *Apprehensive* because past conversations ended badly.
- *Exposed* by the foolish or angry things that you might say.
- *Threatened* by someone else's potential reaction.
- *Unwanted* by the person you're trying to engage.

Can you relate to any of those fears or feelings? I can. You could easily add a number of others to the list, some of which would probably describe you even better. In a sin-saturated world, there are so many variations on the common themes of self-protection and self-absorption that keep us from starting helpful conversations with our children.

The end result, however, is the same: by not talking with your kids you're setting them up to believe things about the world that aren't true. That unintentional deception happens when you don't engage them, when you back off and don't say things that they really need to hear. It also happens when you do engage them, but you reshape the truth to make it easier for you to say or because you think it makes your point more strongly.

Whether you withhold the truth or spin the truth, you present to your child a false picture of the world. You miscommunicate reality to them. That's bad. What's worse is that by doing so, you invite them to interact with that false picture as if it were true. They then attempt to think about, speak into, or act and react to a world that doesn't exist, though they think it does— a world that you helped construct by omitting the truth or by corrupting it.

That's how people end up auditioning for *American Idol*, when they really shouldn't. Have you ever listened to some of the tryouts where an ardent, intense, hopeful soloist is singing her heart out, and there's no polite way to put it, but she's just awful? Have you wondered how that happens?

I know that I can't sing well, so I don't need a televised opportunity to prove it. Apparently others do. But that makes me think to myself as I listen to these auditions, "Wow . . . don't you have any friends? Someone who would lovingly pull you aside and say, 'Look, you're a beautiful person with a wide range of talents, but this just isn't one of them. Please don't embarrass yourself by pursuing this publicly.'"

Why didn't anyone do that for these hopeful people? Surely someone stood next to them while they sang "Happy Birthday" or overheard them singing as they walked from room to room through the house or went with them to a karaoke party and realized this wasn't one of their gifts.

And we're not talking about one or two people who are just odd ducks. We're talking about a significant number of people who are embarrassingly off-key, yet willing to try out anyway. Why didn't someone tell them the truth?

Because of the reasons listed above. Because people are afraid of hurting their friend's feelings. Or they're worried about their friend's possible reaction. Or they hate the idea of an awkward conversation. Or they're concerned that the relationship might lose some of its closeness. And so they don't engage their friend honestly because they think the alternative will keep life running the way they want it to.

That's the point of trimming the truth. You look down the road and assess what might happen if you were to speak honestly and if, in your opinion, doing so might jeopardize something you really want, then you don't.

Dissembling starts early. I think of the little boy who claims to have brushed his teeth when he hasn't so that he can keep playing. He wants to protect his fun. He knows that if he's honest, then he'll have to do something that's not fun and so he lies and invites his parent to enter a fantasy world of his making.

Or consider the little person who lies about sneaking cookies before dinner because she wants dessert afterward. She's protecting something she wants by constructing an imaginary, hence false, world for her parent.

It only gets worse as people get older. I remember the college student who told her parents that she was no longer seeing a certain young man although she still was, because they didn't approve of her choice. She was afraid that the truth would spur her parents to pressure her to end the relationship that she still wanted.

Or there's the young man whose wife left, but he continued to let everyone else believe they were still together because if other people knew, then it would ruin his image. So he omitted the truth to guard his reputation, afraid of what others might think or do if they knew the reality of his life.

I don't need to ask if you can relate to any of these people. I know you can. Every single person on earth knows firsthand what it is to distort reality for the sake of guarding something they want. You may not have intended to lie, but either by what you said, didn't say, or the way you said it, you communicated a world that doesn't exist and invited someone to live in it anyway. It's bad enough when you do that with other adults. It's far worse with your children, who are just learning how to understand the world and their place in it.

Here's the good news: you're not alone. Some of God's closest friends have produced utter chaos in their lives by doing the very same thing you have done: presented a distorted picture of reality for other people to engage. What do you need if that's you? What do you need if you don't want to speak up or speak truthfully when you know you need to?

You need hope. Hope that you have not so ruined your relationships that they're beyond repair or redemption. And hope that you can grow to learn a different way of conversing that's better for the people around you. That means you need to know that someone else who is bigger than you and better than you is involved with you as you talk to your children.

The account of Abraham as he lies to others in Genesis 20 is that story of hope. It's a great case study that we'll examine over the next few chapters.

Genesis 20

From there [by the oaks of Mamre (Gen. 18:1)] Abraham journeyed toward the territory of the Negeb and lived between Kadesh and Shur; and he sojourned in Gerar. And Abraham said of Sarah his wife, "She is my sister." And Abimelech king of Gerar sent and took Sarah. But God came to Abimelech in a dream by night and said to him, "Behold, you are a dead man because of the woman whom you have taken, for she is a man's wife." Now Abimelech had not approached her. So he said, "Lord, will you kill an innocent people? Did he not himself say to me, 'She is my sister'? And she herself said, 'He is my brother.' In the integrity of my heart and the innocence of my hands I have done this." Then God said to him in the dream, "Yes, I know that you have done this in the integrity of your heart, and it was I who kept you from sinning against me. Therefore I did not let you touch her. Now then, return the man's wife, for he is a prophet, so that he will pray for you, and you shall live. But if you do not return her, know that you shall surely die, you and all who are yours."

So Abimelech rose early in the morning and called all his servants and told them all these things. And the men were very much afraid. Then Abimelech called Abraham and said to him, "What have you done to us? And how have I sinned against you, that you have brought on me and my kingdom a great sin? You have done to me things that ought not to be done." And Abimelech said to Abraham, "What did you see, that you did this thing?" Abraham said, "I did it because I thought, 'There is no fear of God at all in this place, and they will kill me because of my wife.' Besides, she is indeed my sister, the daughter of my father though not the daughter of my mother, and she became my wife. And when God caused me to wander from my father's house, I said to her,

'This is the kindness you must do me: at every place to which we come, say of me, "He is my brother."'"

Then Abimelech took sheep and oxen, and male servants and female servants, and gave them to Abraham, and returned Sarah his wife to him. And Abimelech said, "Behold, my land is before you; dwell where it pleases you." To Sarah he said, "Behold, I have given your brother a thousand pieces of silver. It is a sign of your innocence in the eyes of all who are with you, and before everyone you are vindicated." Then Abraham prayed to God, and God healed Abimelech, and also healed his wife and female slaves so that they bore children. For the LORD had closed all the wombs of the house of Abimelech because of Sarah, Abraham's wife.

11

Abraham Misspeaks for God

Abraham lied about his wife. He had just moved into a new region and was scared. He assumed—rightly or wrongly—that if people knew Sarah was his wife, then they might try to kill him to get at her. From that starting point he reasoned, "If no one thinks she's my wife, then there's no reason to kill me." True, but his reasoning didn't go far enough. He didn't realize that far from removing people's interest in Sarah, the opposite had to happen; their interest would only increase since there was no reason for them not to be interested.

The upshot is that Abraham found himself in a very uncomfortable place with Abimelech. We don't know how, but Sarah caught Abimelech's attention, and he wanted her, so he sent for her.

Now keep in mind that Abraham had enough servants to field an army of 318 men who defeated the combined military might of four kings (Gen. 14:11–16). He's not the kind of man you'd casually start a war with, which makes me wonder if Abimelech diplomatically made overtures to Abraham to discuss marrying his "sister." That would have been uncomfortable for Abraham—but no more difficult than when Abimelech sent for Sarah.

Whether there were advance conversations or not, it's clear that Abimelech didn't know the true nature of the couple's relationship. That means Abraham kept silent. Even if he didn't verbally encourage Abimelech, he didn't publically disagree. And he should have. At some point as things unfolded, it became well past time for Abraham to clear his throat and say, "Um, this is awkward, but you know what? I'm sorry. I lied."

But he didn't. And so Abimelech sent for Sarah, forcing Abraham to face an impossible situation of his own making. Now he had to talk with his wife. Can you imagine him saying, "Gee, honey, I've got some bad news"? What went through his mind as he watched her pack her belongings and leave their tent to go live with another man?

As you think through the process, you realize that Abraham's lie was not a one-off, spur-of-the-moment kind of thing. Not only had he planned it out in advance, but he had multiple opportunities to retract it and didn't take any of them. Fear is powerful. Once you start down the road of deception, it is hard to do anything but keep on going.

And the effects keep rippling outward. Abraham misrepresented reality to Abimelech, and Abimelech, instead of responding to the way things really were, responded to what he'd been told. Since he thought Sarah was Abraham's sister, he didn't see anything wrong with thinking she was available. Abraham's small, "protect-me" lie affected not just him and his household, but everyone around him.

That's one reason why lies are wrong; they don't love your neighbor. They don't care about anyone else's well-being. They present a false view of the world as though it were true and then invite those around you to interact with that false world. When the picture you create for others isn't true, you're setting people up to act in a way that certainly will harm both them and you in the process. Lies always have a cost even if initially they don't seem so bad.

Abraham was now feeling the cost. Sarah certainly knew the cost. But frankly, the whole world was about to pay. It's pretty clear by this point in Genesis that the promised child is to come through the union of Abraham and Sarah (Gen. 17:15–22). That child would father the people of God from whom ultimately the Messiah, who would save his people and crush Satan's head (Gen. 3:15), would come. With Sarah leaving Abraham's tent, that promised child is now in jeopardy. That's a huge cost that Abraham never considered.

Abraham's lie, however, also costs God, but to see that price you have to step back and look at the big picture. Remember, God originally made people in his image so that they could be a visible picture of the invisible God to the rest of creation, representing him to everything and everyone around them (Gen. 1:26–28).

That's why rebellion in the garden of Eden is so vile. God's images rejected God's ways in God's world, choosing instead to follow another voice. And in that instant they exchanged their privilege of reflecting the glory of God for mirroring the ugliness of the serpent.

The next several chapters in Genesis detail how the story of humanity goes from bad to worse as evil increases in breadth and depth, spreading across the earth and infiltrating every human heart.

- The blame-shifting of chapter 3 gives way to murder in chapter 4.
- Chapter 6 explains that evil is so deeply rooted in humanity that every inclination of the human heart is only evil all the time (Gen. 6:5). God responds with the cleansing judgment of the flood (Genesis 6–9), but even that catastrophe doesn't change our sin-infected condition (Gen. 9:18–28).
- Chapter 11 closes off this section of Genesis by noting that the human race had devolved as far as possible from our original mandate to fill the earth with the image of God (Gen. 1:28). Rather than spreading out across the globe to proclaim the glory of God, people gathered together in one city, Babel, to make a name for themselves (Gen. 11:4).

Then you turn the page to chapter 12, and you are introduced to a very underwhelming person: Abraham. A nomad wandering around in the middle of the wilderness. A nobody. But do you remember what God calls Abraham as he confronts Abimelech? He's a prophet (Gen. 20:7). Abraham is someone who speaks for God. He's completely unknown and unremarkable, but God decided that here is the person through whom he's going to make himself known. If you hear Abraham, you hear God. He's the new Adam.

And this person with such a high calling, to be God's representative, opens his mouth and speaks just like the serpent. Jesus will later call Satan a liar from the beginning and the father of lies (John 8:44), and here's Abraham, God's new representative, speaking lies, sounding just like the snake. He's ruined his own family and put Abimelech and his family at risk, but worse than all of that, he's misrepresented God to the cosmos.

It's tragic. God is working to redeem the horror of Eden, and Abraham is working to recreate it.

Can you relate? Have there been times when you've represented the serpent better than you've represented your Creator? Times when you have reshaped the truth out of fear that something would happen that you didn't want? You lied about where you were or who you were with. You lied about where you were going or what you did when you got there. You actively painted a picture that made people look in the wrong direction.

It happens on the grand scales of Genesis 20. It happens daily on the most trivial levels. I was in a class where the professor was trying to hold a group discussion, only no one was saying much, so he asked, "Did you guys do the reading for this week?" No one responded, so he looked right at me and asked again, "How much of the reading did you do?"

And I looked him right in the eye and said, "Most" (by which I meant that any day now I'd be closing in on about 51 percent). Only, I knew that he would interpret "most" to be closer to 90 percent, and that's what I wanted him to think. I intentionally misrepresented God in that moment. I misdirected another image of God so that he would still think I was a good student. It's so easy to misrepresent God by what you say and by what you leave unsaid. You know your wife would be hurt or angry over the Internet sites you visited, so you don't bother telling her. Or you know your husband would challenge what you spent, so you keep it from him and you use cash instead of your credit card. Or there have been times when you don't correct your boss but you allow him to believe that your part of the project will be done earlier than it possibly could be.

Leaving things unsaid that you should say makes complete sense, but only if your goal is to invite people to think better of you than they should. It doesn't take long, however, to learn that these passive ways of misrepresenting God are just as deadly as the active ones. Any time you set out to represent the thankless, self-centered serpent who helped ruin the garden, you can expect similar ruin in your own life.

That's the road Abraham set himself on as he actively and passively misrepresented God to Abimelech. Sadly, that road is all too common. What's amazing is the uncommon person who reached out to help Abraham on that road.

12

God Speaks for Abraham

How would you respond to Abraham's betrayal if you were God? I would be tempted to let him have it—"What do you think you're doing? Look at all I'm trying to do to rescue the human race and look at all I've promised you personally. If I couldn't keep you alive, I certainly wouldn't have sworn on my own life to give you a child and a place for your family to live (Gen. 15:12–21). Where's the faith you're so well known for (Rom. 4:3; Heb. 11:8–10; James 2:23)? If you had even an ounce of backbone, then we wouldn't be in this mess!"

Or maybe you're not the exploding kind. Maybe you'd be more tempted to sigh in frustration and throw up your hands—"Okay, Abraham, you've made your bed, now you'll just have to lie in it . . . alone. It's time you felt some consequences for what you've done. Maybe losing Sarah is what you need to wake you up."

Or worse—"You know what? I don't have time for this nonsense. I have a world to save, and you're not helping at all. I'm going to have to put you on the back shelf while I look for someone else who can represent me better."

God doesn't do anything like that. He doesn't sit back. He acts. He gets involved. He initiates. But he doesn't go to Abraham to make him feel guilty so that he'll man up and go do the right thing and stand up for himself. Nor does God bawl him out for letting him down. Actually, he doesn't go to Abraham at all. He goes to Abimelech to start setting things right that are wrong.

The contrast between God and Abraham is dramatic. Abraham had more than enough time to act and didn't, while God doesn't waste any time. He moves quickly to confront Abimelech before he gets near Sarah or touches her (Gen. 20:4, 6). He is more involved in Abraham's life than Abraham is.

This is not a God who has a hands-off policy in running his world. He cares about what happens to people, especially his people—and especially those who work hard to ruin their lives—and he acts on his concern. He cares about you and the mess you've made of your life even more than you do.

When you see what God does for Abraham, you realize it costs him to get involved. What does God do? He speaks to Abimelech. He talks. That's very important in this context. Don't let yourself gloss over what's taking place here. God takes words that Abimelech will understand and uses them to convey not a misshapen picture of reality, but a picture of how the world really is—of who Sarah really is and what will happen to Abimelech and those who are connected to him if he doesn't make things right.

God initiated a conversation to restore Sarah to Abraham. He used his mouth to talk about things that were in Abraham's best interests. He spoke truthfully so that Abimelech could have an accurate picture of what? Of Abraham. God didn't talk about himself, but represented Abraham and his interests to Abimelech. God reversed roles and became Abraham's prophet. That's humility. He became Abraham's mouthpiece, speaking what was right and true of Abraham and his life.

In that moment, you see God's heart. He didn't speak up because it would enrich his own world or make things better for himself. He could have found someone else to take Abraham's place as the father of many nations (Gen. 17:4). But he didn't

want someone else. That's why he bound and obligated himself
to Abraham (Gen. 15:8–21).

Having done so, he then spoke for Abraham's sake, to make
Abraham's life better. He cares for his people, even for those who
don't deserve it—for those who have misrepresented him in the
way they act toward others. He doesn't hold your failures against
you, but acts even when you're not right to bring about a life that
is better for you than the one you chose for yourself.

Notice that doesn't always mean a life that is easy. God's
speaking for Abraham meant that Abraham had to have a very
difficult conversation with Abimelech (Gen. 20:9–13). He had to
own up to what he had done to Abimelech and Sarah along with
the cowardly reasons behind it. That wasn't easy, but true to God's
redemptive longings, there's glory even in the act of owning the
ugly things he did.

As Abraham confessed his sin along with what prodded him
into lying, he reflected the God of truth by accurately speaking
about what he'd done wrong. In that moment, he took back his
role of representing God by speaking honestly about the way the
world is instead of trying to hide things from other people. Even
when God's representatives don't live rightly, God makes a way
for them to handle their failures in a way that can honor him.
Don't ever take this lightly: God will always make some way for
you to live righteously even after you have just been faithless.

The point of the account is not that God works to reshape
the world so you can have the life you want. The point is that his
work in your life restores you to the place you were always meant
to have in his world.

Did you notice, however, that he did more than simply restore
Abraham to his truth-telling role? He reinstated his ministry. God
did not come to Abimelech and tell him to return Sarah and say
that everything would be okay in his family after that. Abimelech
still needed Abraham to pray for him. Abraham regained the role
that he had abandoned earlier.

God did not say to him, "Okay, Abraham, I get that this is too much for you. Just sit back, and I'll take it from here." Instead God involved himself so that Abraham resumed his rightful place on the earth, interceding for Abimelech and for his family. He once again took words to God on behalf of other people (Gen. 20:17). God spoke up for Abraham so that Abraham could take back his place as God's prophet.

That sounds really hopeful until it occurs to you to ask, "But what if I'm not as special as Abraham?" No doubt you can relate to his sin as you've used words to misrepresent God and reality to your children. But I suspect you've not had the same kind of experience Abraham did where God appeared and obligated himself to you (Gen. 15:9–21).

So what hope do you have when you've misused your mouth? That question underlines just how important it is that you see how this account, like all of Scripture, finds its fulfillment in Christ.

13

Jesus Speaks for You

Abraham proved he was not the new, flawless Adam—the one who in perfectly representing God to the cosmos would be the forerunner and founder of a new race of humans like himself. But Jesus is. That's why theologians call him "the second Adam." When he walked on earth, he perfectly represented God in everything he did and said. He was *the* image of God. When you saw and heard him, you saw and heard God.

But Jesus did more than just bring God to humans. He also brought humans before God. He took words back to God to represent humans, interceding on their behalf. He prayed for his friends—for their well-being and for when they struggled (Luke 22:32; John 17:9, 15). He even prayed for those who hated him (Luke 23:34), living out what he taught about praying for your enemies (Matt. 5:44; Luke 6:28).

Jesus, the Word of God made flesh—physically manifesting God's voice to humanity—also took words to God on behalf of flesh. He represented his friends to God and lobbied for their best interests in the throne room of heaven.

Not only did he speak for a handful of people two thousand years ago, but even then he was thinking about and including you in his prayers (John 17:20). And he continues serving you by taking words to the Father even now as your present High Priest in heaven, who "is able to save to the uttermost those who draw near to God through him, since he always lives to make intercession for them" (Heb. 7:25; see also Rom. 8:34). Or as his friend John put it: "But if anyone does sin, we have an advocate with the Father, Jesus Christ the righteous" (1 John 2:1). Jesus is our advocate, one who speaks to the Father in our defense.

In other words, Scripture writers had a sense of Jesus carrying out an ongoing prayer ministry. They knew that our struggle on this earth with sin is of the life-long, never-ending variety. While we're no longer controlled by sin, it still makes its presence felt daily and hourly, which means that we need regular, long-term care that matches the regular, long-term nature of our problem.

If you wrestled with a chronic physical condition and discovered a health care provider who promised new treatment options, you might feel some hope, some sense of "Finally! Now maybe we'll get somewhere." But if that person and his treatments can't or won't continue to hang in there with you and keep making a difference to your condition, then they create an added burden. You feel even more demoralized and hopeless than you were before.

Jesus doesn't add that burden to you. He stays with you, giving you ongoing help. He keeps interceding for you as you struggle, even though he doesn't have to. Think about it. He entered your life with a dramatic, breakthrough intervention. On the cross he took your sin and gave you his righteous standing with God. He then poured out his Spirit in you to teach you and strengthen you to live well. Isn't that enough? He would be more than justified to sit back and let you struggle through the rest of life on your own.

But he doesn't. He doesn't abandon you, grow tired of working with you, feel overwhelmed by you, get discouraged or go looking for someone who's more likely to be successful.

He doesn't berate you. He doesn't pull away in shocked horror. He doesn't say, "Gee, I wonder what you're going to do now?" He doesn't even wait for you to figure out that you've got a problem.

Instead he stays close to you, dedicated to providing ongoing care by interceding for you. He makes sure that the cure he began works fully and completely so that one day you will no longer be plagued by sin, but be fully and completely whole.

That means you are not alone when you sin. Jesus speaks to the Father for you, often before you know that you've got a problem. He goes to the King of all the universe and talks to him on your account. He intercedes for you along with the Holy Spirit, who speaks for you with groans that words cannot express (Rom. 8:26).

And that's exactly what I need when I misrepresent God. I don't need to try harder to make up for what I did wrong, hoping I'll get it right the next time so he'll cut me some slack. And I don't need to run away from the mess I made when I don't know what to do with it. Instead, I need to run back to my High Priest with confidence and ask him to restore me even though I've failed miserably again.

That's something I have more experience with than I'd like to admit. Years ago one of our sons had decided that living under my wife's and my direction in our home wasn't his best option. When we tried to step into his life and redirect him to what we thought was best, we were met with looks of boredom, anger, or a fake smile that was intended to let us know just how little he thought of our input. Then he'd disappear into another room to do what he wanted—watch TV, read a book, or play a video game—until he wanted something from us. Then he would come back to test the water to see if we were still upset.

As hours of struggling with his approach to us turned into days that turned into weeks with no perceivable movement or change, I got fed up. I could feel my temper become increasingly shorter as time went on. I was less willing to put up with things I didn't like. I became more critical, noticing all the things he was doing wrong and letting fewer and fewer of them slide. I got louder.

And I felt justified. I had tried to be reasonable, and he just wasn't getting it. That's when I started to pull back. I found myself doing all the things that God's representatives don't do—I would avoid being in the same room with him or pretend I didn't see him when he was there. Sometimes I pretended I didn't hear him. And still nothing changed.

But instead of talking to him, I talked to myself—only the words inside my head didn't reflect the good God who talks to me when I ignore his direction. My internal conversation sounded more like, "What is wrong with him? He's not doing anything different. He doesn't care. We keep talking and talking and he keeps ignoring us, living like he can do whatever he wants. Why should I put up with this? I work way too hard to have to deal with this when I get home every day. I don't deserve this. He needs to treat me better in my house after all I do for him."

Do you know the problem with holding those internal dialogues in your mind? They don't stay there. They start to leak out around the edges. You start to look more and more upset. You don't smile at the person you're thinking about.

You stop saying "I love you" when you see the person because in your mind you're saying, "Love you? Right now I don't even like you." That's when you know you're in danger because it would be so easy to say, "I don't like you" out loud. You've been rehearsing those words in your mind so long, they start to sound right. They match the way you feel, and it would be so easy to speak them . . . but doing so would misrepresent God in that moment. You would communicate to someone—made in the image of God—"You're only loveable when you're likeable. You're only worth my time and energy when you're nice to be around. If you can't be good to me, then you can forget having any kind of relationship with me."

Thankfully, God is not like that. He doesn't say things like that, because he doesn't think things like that—not even when I'm about to misrepresent him to my son. So I confessed to God: "I'm not representing you well right now. I've gotten tired of trying to do the right thing, and now I'm only making things worse. Please forgive me and please restore me to being the kind of dad you've always meant me to be. Oh, and by the way, thank you for interceding for me even before I realized I was in trouble."

That prayer didn't straighten out everything in my home; it started to straighten out things in my heart. I felt myself softening toward my son. I wanted to talk with him and try one more time. So we sat down together, and I said, "I'm sure you've noticed over the past several weeks that I've been less patient with you and more critical and that I've pulled away. I know there are many reasons for why I've been doing that, but the bottom line is that I'm wrong and I want to ask you to forgive me." And he did.

Now you might expect me to say that everything with him became warm and fuzzy after that moment. It didn't. It didn't even become warm and fuzzy the rest of that day. But there was a profound difference. I was different. I still had to address a number of things in him that I saw, but I did so with more patience. I initiated again. I noticed him, talked to him, hugged him, and told him, "I do love you."

And that made a difference. Life has not been easy for him and me, but that afternoon helped by rebuilding a context for us to have the harder conversations that we needed—a context where I could represent Christ to him instead of the serpent. That context has helped him understand that I'm not his enemy—that I'm not cutting him out of my life when he doesn't behave rightly.

That's the kind of Christ you have. He descends into the mess of your life in order to restore you so that you can enter into the mess of the lives of the people around you. Before you can help others deal with their messes, however, you have to deal with your own first. The next chapter explains how.

14

You Take Words to God

Jesus has taken words to God on your behalf when you have wrongly spoken to your children. Now it's your turn to take words to God. We've seen from Abraham's life that there are two problems when you misuse your mouth: you not only sin against people by painting a false picture of reality, but more importantly you sin against the God who sculpted you in his image.

While you need to address both problems, there is an order for how you go about it. First, you need to be restored to God so that you reflect him accurately. Only then are you ready, secondly, to be restored to your fellow image-bearer. Thankfully, even if your child doesn't want to reconnect with you, God guarantees that he himself does.

His guarantee is counterintuitive, if you think about it. After all, the problem with him is so much bigger than with your child. You might not have thought about it, but by sinning against him, you've created a problem of infinite proportions.

- When you misrepresent an infinite person, there is no limit to the damage you've done to his reputation.
- Consider it from a different perspective: just as two nonparallel lines end up infinitely far apart, the slightest deviation

from a perfectly righteous God, if it goes uncorrected, will result in an infinite chasm between the two of you.

• Or take into account that his infinite holiness is guarded by his infinite wrath that demands his infinite justice. Does that start to give you a sense of how big the problem is that you've created?

When you reflect the serpent, rather than the Creator, to others, you're not merely being a broken person. You're inflicting that brokenness on others and expanding it into his world, only to discover that you'll never be big enough to fix the damage or make things right. How can you hope to be restored to him?

You hope because he invites you back to himself. Here's how:

> Return, Israel, to the Lord your God.
>   Your sins have been your downfall!
> Take words with you
>   and return to the Lord.
> Say to him:
>   "Forgive all our sins
> and receive us graciously,
>   that we may offer the fruit of our lips.
> Assyria cannot save us;
>   we will not mount warhorses.
> We will never again say 'Our gods'
>   to what our own hands have made,
>   for in you the fatherless find compassion."
>   (Hos. 14:1–3 NIV)

That's amazing. Your words have been your problem, estranging you from him, and now his words propose that your words become the vehicle to reunite you with him. Jesus never stopped taking words to the Father for you. As a follower of Christ, you take words as well. And they're very simple words:

• A simple request that the Father not make you pay for what you've done: *"Forgive all."*

- An unvarnished acknowledgement that there is something to pay: *"our sins."*
- A longing not to be rejected by him: *"and receive us graciously."*
- A desire to use words well: *"that we may offer the fruit of our lips."*
- An awareness that nothing else can save you from yourself: *"Assyria cannot save us . . . [nor our] warhorses . . . [or even] what our own hands have made."*
- A reminder that you depend on his love despite having worked so hard to earn his judgment: *"for in you the fatherless find compassion."*

Simple words can restore the rift you've made, but only because he's invited you to bring them: *"Take words with you and return to the LORD."* He didn't cause the problem, but he has a solution. You can't fix the breakdown between the two of you, but he will. And yet, you still have a part to play. Your part is to say to him, "I want it fixed. I broke our relationship, but I don't want it to stay broken."

It would be presumptive arrogance to say that to him without an invitation; with one, however, it would be madness not to. Here's his heart: he still wants you. He still wants a friendship with you. The question is, Do you want him? The way you know is by whether you take him up on his offer or not, by whether you take words to him.

When you do, you join a long line of people who also came to their senses and returned to him because they had hope that he still wanted them. People who realized, despite all their worst mistakes, that God would welcome them back when they confessed the evil they had done. People who knew how to say, "We have sinned" (e.g., Judg. 10:10; 1 Sam. 7:6; 2 Sam. 12:13; 24:10; Pss. 41:4; 51; Jer. 14:7).

It's no accident that as the wayward son in one of Jesus's stories returns to his long-suffering father, he begins with a simple confession: "Father, I have sinned against heaven and before you" (Luke 15:21). Jesus knew that the Father's heart invites people to bring words of repentance to him. That heart would have made sense to anyone familiar with Israel's history and architecture. The original temple was a visual reminder that institutionalized God's invitation. Read through Solomon's dedicatory prayer of the temple in 1 Kings 8:22–53, and you'll discover that God's forgiveness was being offered to people who would take simple words of confession to God when they had sinned against him (1 Kings 8:33–34, 35–36, 46–51).

The temple was God's invitation literally set in stone. He couldn't make it any more permanent until Jesus came to replace the impermanent stones that housed the impermanent altar on which impermanent priests offered impermanent sacrifices. Only his never-ending, enduring self could replace them all. That's why we now confess our sins to him, knowing that since he is faithful and just, he will forgive us our sins and purify us from all unrighteousness (1 John 1:9). He will restore us to himself.

And you need that restoration experience, not only so that you can say righteous things to your children, but so that you keep in mind what you're really hoping for after you finish talking with them. You're hoping that just like you, they too will want to talk to the same God who invited you to talk with him.

15

Practice Repenting for Misusing Your Mouth

~~Most highly exalted God . . .~~
~~You who were, long before time began . . .~~
~~Merciful and Holy Father . . .~~
Dad . . .

I broke something today that's really important to me, and I don't know if it can be fixed, but I do know that I can't fix it.

I said something really stupid. I was tired. It was a bad day. I wasn't feeling well, but none of those were the real problem. The real problem is worse. My kid was getting in the way of what I wanted. It didn't seem so bad at the time. I just wanted them:

- to listen
- to stop arguing
- to get off my back
- to give me a break
- to not be so annoying
- to stop demanding everything in the store
- to care about their mother/father/brother/sister
- to be thankful for what they got

- to think about me for a change
- to do what I asked
- to lighten up
- to just let me sit quietly for five minutes
- to get on board with what the rest of the family was doing
- to stop complaining
- to have some consideration for someone besides themselves
- to let me watch my show

It seemed like such a small thing to ask for at the time. But when I hear what I said, it's obvious that I wanted it more than I wanted anything else in the world. And because they weren't giving me what I wanted—what I thought they owed me—I took your gift of words and used them like the Enemy does. Only, now, I wish I hadn't.

I can't take my words back, but you have said that you will forgive me because Jesus paid for every misspoken word I have ever said. It's hard for me to imagine how that's even possible, but you have never misused your words with me or anyone else, and so I believe what you say.

Please forgive me and don't count my words against me or throw them back in my face or use them against me.

Thank you for inviting me to talk to you about this—it's amazing to me that you'd want to hear anything that comes out of my mouth after what I've said, but I think that means that I'm still learning what it means to be forgiven.

Thank you. Thank you for forgiving me. Thank you that one day this will not be a problem we need to talk about. Thank you for the day that is coming when I will never say another thing that's out of line or that I regret. Seriously, Dad, I can't wait.

And please teach me to talk like you do. I want to learn. I need to go back to my kids now, and I'm not at all sure what to say. I need to ask their forgiveness and that will be hard, but it will be even harder to know what to say next.

Will you please talk to me through your Spirit so that I know how to talk to my children? It's really cool how you parent me into being a better parent. Please give me thoughts and ideas to put into words. And please keep my ears open to hear how you're talking to me. I don't want you to ever stop. I like being your child. Thanks.

16

You Hear Words from God

As necessary as it is for you to take words to God, your greater need is to hear words from him because of how easy it is to be tempted to think you've damaged your relationship with him beyond repair.

It's odd, but before you say or do something wrong, you rarely consider how it might affect you and him. It's only after you see what you've done that the relational questions come flooding in:

- Is he angry and upset with me?
- Will we ever be as close as we used to be?
- How long will he hold this thing against me?
- Is he going to bring it back up again?
- When is he going to get tired of putting up with me?

Thankfully, God understands how you're tempted to believe he won't handle your failings well, and so he speaks in different ways throughout Scripture:

- He reminds you that he still warmly accepts and embraces you.
- He invites you to trust him when you've not been trustworthy.

- He gives you confidence that he still wants you when you've wandered away.
- He underlines that he remains faithful to you when you've been faithless.
- He tells you that he doesn't relate to you according to how bad you've been, but according to how good he is.

These reassurances from God are crucial to helping you realize that the strength of your relationship depends on his goodness far more than it does on yours. That's hard to believe sometimes though, especially when you feel the gulf between what you've done and what you know you should have done.

When my son Timmy was ten years old, he was talking with me in the kitchen and agonizing over his salvation and whether he was doing all the right things, like reading his Bible and praying, and whether he was doing them enough.

It was one of those moments when I realized that words alone didn't have the power to break through. So without warning, I swooped down and grabbed both of his legs then stood back up, holding him upside down in the air.

He laughed and whooped, but also started flailing around, trying to find a way to grab onto me to make sure he didn't fall. After half a minute or so I quieted him down and asked, "Are you falling?"

"No," he giggled.

I continued, "So, right now, what do you think is most true—that you're not falling because you're holding on to me or because I'm holding on to you?" I loved that he actually had to pause and think about it before he answered me. Suspended upside down in the air, holding on to absolutely nothing, he was still conditioned to believe that his life was okay primarily because of what he was doing. That's a great picture of how we often relate to our heavenly Father—believing that we are more responsible than he is for how good things are between us.

Thankfully, it took only a few moments for Tim to realize, "You're holding on to me." It was a brand-new way of thinking about life, but he got it.

I put him down—right side up—then bent down on one knee and said, "That's what's true of your friendship with Jesus too. He holds on to you much harder than you will ever hold on to him. You don't need to worry so much about whether you're doing all the right things or not, because the strength of your relationship with him primarily depends on him. Not on you. That's why he died for you. He's a lot better at holding on to you than you ever will be at holding on to him."

The next time you're tempted to worry that you've set your relationship with God back because of what you've said or done to someone, you need to hear God say to you that he holds you more tightly than you hold him.

How do you do that? Try this: pick a book of the Bible and start reading it, not to highlight God's commands or people's failures, but to hear God's relational reassurances, which you'll often find in response to someone's failure. When you listen like this, you'll hear things that will give you greater confidence in him. Things like:

- "Come now, let us reason together, says the LORD: / though your sins are like scarlet, / they shall be as white as snow; / though they are red like crimson, / they shall become like wool." (Isa. 1:18)
- The LORD passed before [Moses] and proclaimed, "The LORD, the LORD, a God merciful and gracious, slow to anger, and abounding in steadfast love and faithfulness, keeping steadfast love for thousands, forgiving iniquity and transgression and sin. (Ex. 34:6–7)
- The LORD your God is in your midst, / a mighty one who will save; / he will rejoice over you with gladness; / he will quiet you by his love; / he will exult over you with loud singing. (Zeph. 3:17)

- [Jesus said,] "All that the Father gives me will come to me, and whoever comes to me I will never cast out." (John 6:37)

These are the kinds of things you can expect God to say and the attitude he has when you're wrestling with your own struggles. Alternatively, as you're reading, make a list of the things that people in Scripture tell you about their experience of God or how they urge you to relate to him. Both give you a glimpse of his heart, which continues to welcome people who don't always get things right. Listen to people who know they are still wanted so you learn that you are too:

> The LORD is merciful and gracious,
>> slow to anger and abounding in steadfast love.
> He will not always chide,
>> nor will he keep his anger forever.
> He does not deal with us according to our sins,
>> nor repay us according to our iniquities.
> For as high as the heavens are above the earth,
>> so great is his steadfast love toward those who
>> fear him;
> as far as the east is from the west,
>> so far does he remove our transgressions from us.
>> (Ps. 103:8–12)

If we confess our sins, he is faithful and just to forgive us our sins and to cleanse us from all unrighteousness. (1 John 1:9)

> The sacrifices of God are a broken spirit;
>> a broken and contrite heart, O God, you will not despise.
>> (Ps. 51:17)

Draw near to God, and he will draw near to you. (James 4:8)

> If we are faithless, he remains faithful—
> for he cannot deny himself. (2 Tim. 2:13)

As you meditate on these words from God to you, you can't help but grow in confidence that he's holding you because he wants you—even in those moments when you wouldn't want you. His words will give you courage to reenter relationships with your kids, even relationships that you've damaged. And you'll reengage your kids with the hope that you now have what it takes to speak well to them: an ongoing experience of someone who keeps speaking well to you.

17

You Take Words to Your Kids

Having taken words to God and having heard words from him, you now take those same kinds of words to your children. That's the dynamic Paul describes in his letter to the Ephesians. He reminds them how amazing it is that they've been brought into God's family (chaps. 1–2), but then he points out how much they have to learn now that they're part of it (chaps. 4–6). Want to guess how that growth happens? You're right. Most of it comes through conversations that they have with other family members (e.g., Eph. 4:15, 21, 25, 29; 5:19; 6:4, 21–22).

Notice in the following section from Ephesians 4 that there are only two potential futures for his family: we can become mature or we can remain childish.

And he gave the apostles, the prophets, the evangelists, the shepherds and teachers, to equip the saints for the work of ministry, for building up the body of Christ, until we all attain to the unity of the faith and of the knowledge of the Son of God, to mature manhood, to the measure of the stature of the fullness of Christ, so that we may no longer be children, tossed to and fro by the waves and carried about by every wind of doctrine, by human cunning, by craftiness in deceitful schemes.

Rather, speaking the truth in love, we are to grow up in every way into him who is the head, into Christ, from whom the whole body, joined and held together by every joint with which it is equipped, when each part is working properly, makes the body grow so that it builds itself up in love. (Eph. 4:11–16)

God's family can flounder aimlessly, like a wave at sea subject to any and all passing breezes, or his family can grow up. Childish or mature: those are our options. And a key element in determining that outcome is how we talk to one another. Since our smaller families are modeled on God's larger one, the way ours will grow is the same way that his does.

The question then is, Do you want a family that is mature? If so, you need to talk to the people in it like God's people are urged to talk to each other. You need to say things that will build relationships rather than destroy them. Things like: "Let no corrupting talk come out of your mouths, but only such as is good for building up, as fits the occasion, that it may give grace to those who hear" (Eph. 4:29).

Take that sentence apart phrase by phrase, and you'll see the beauty in it.

- Everything I say needs to be *good for building* others up. Every joke I tell, every tidbit of news I relay, the things I share from my day, my comments on someone's haircut, the way I coach, the kind of help I give with homework, my appreciation of dinner, my expressions of gratitude for how others pitch in around the house—everything I say needs to work at building up the people around me.
- Everything I say needs to *fit the occasion*, or as the NIV puts it, that it be *according to what others need*. That doesn't mean I say what people want to hear, but that my words are guided by what others need to hear. Before I open my mouth, I have to consider what is necessary in this moment for someone else to hear.

- Everything I say needs to have a chance to *give grace to those who hear.* Your words must always convey grace to the people around you for the sake of leaving them better off than before you said anything. That's how God talks to you, his child; now you talk with that same intention to your own.

In other words, "corrupting talk" has nothing to do with swearing or telling an off-color joke. *Corrupting* in this context means saying anything that will hurt another person or saying something that won't help.

That's a tall order when I'm at my best, but what happens when I get blindsided by life? What about when I need to say something and I'm not at my best or the other person isn't at his best? That's when this starts to sound impossible, doesn't it?

Notice Paul doesn't say, "Don't say anything"—you might be able to pull that off. Instead, he essentially says, "You don't get to ignore the weeklong war your kids insist on waging in your home. You have to speak. But you can only say what will give them grace."

How is that possible? What if you grew up in an environment that rarely spoke honestly but lovingly for the purpose of leaving others better off? What if you can't remember receiving any grace-filled experiences that you can pass along to anyone else?

I was teaching on this verse once when someone stopped me and asked, "Do you really believe that?" I was a little taken aback. "Do you really believe that the only words coming out of our mouth are to purposely benefit others?"

If you think about it, you can understand why someone would ask that. This sounds like a nice ideal, but one that is completely unrealistic. It resembles one of those simplistic things you'd find in a self-help book: "How to have good relationships with your kids: Step 1: Never Say Anything Unhelpful to Them." And you roll your eyes as you think, "Yeah, okay. I'll get right on that."

It kind of sounds like advice coming from the same camp as "Just say no to drugs." Just say no. And your mind rolls its eyes.

"Oh, Right! What were we thinking all of these years? Who knew it was that easy? Just say no, and all our youth issues will disappear, our inner cities will be cleaned up, and our suburbs will be drug-free."

It's advice that you might agree sounds good if only you didn't personally have a sense of how hard it is to say no: just say no to a second helping of dinner when you don't need to eat any more, but you really liked the food; just say no to dessert afterward; just say no to the really cute sweater you just have to have. Doesn't "only say what is helpful for building others up" feel like it's in the same category?

Here's the difference. This is from God. If someone else said it, you could safely ignore him, but here's God telling you, "Only [say] such as is good for building [others] up." In other words, he believes that your conversations are a key way that people experience grace in their lives or they are a key way that they experience unwholesomeness (the absence of grace). Your words will either help people understand how grace looks and feels—how God himself would speak to them if he were here—or your words will help them understand the hopelessness and meanness of hell.

Now, before you get overwhelmed, you need to realize that Paul is making an assumption in verse 29. He assumes that in order for you to speak grace to others, you have already heard grace yourself. That you have experienced grace and received grace. That you have already had the experience of someone crafting every word he's spoken to you to build you up.

Remember, our words always reflect what we ourselves have heard. It's only as you live in a gracious relationship with God that you gain a sense of what grace sounds like and, therefore, you have a sense of what to say to others. That means you need more than just ideas about life and Christianity.

Obviously knowledge and truth are essential for Christians—that's why Paul spent the first two chapters of his letter focused on theology: who this gracious God is, what he's done, and how that impacts you. But you need more. You need a present experience of this God actively loving you, and no amount of theological doctrine will give you that.

And Paul knows that. So before he focuses on how you need to talk as part of God's family in chapters 4–5, he pauses in chapter 3 and prays for you to have a fresh experience of Jesus living in your heart so that you know and believe how much he loves you.

> For this reason I bow my knees before the Father, from whom every family in heaven and on earth is named, that according to the riches of his glory he may grant you to be strengthened with power through his Spirit in your inner being, so that Christ may dwell in your hearts through faith—that you, being rooted and grounded in love, may have strength to comprehend with all the saints what is the breadth and length and height and depth, and to know the love of Christ that surpasses knowledge, that you may be filled with all the fullness of God. (Eph. 3:14–19)

Keep in mind that Paul is praying for Christians, for people who have received Christ and are part of his family. But his prayer is that, though you already are friends with Jesus, you would experience your friendship in fresh new ways. He prays that you would reexperience Christ living in your heart through faith. That you would have a renewed sense of this God alive in you, actively loving you, being gracious to you. That you would know how great God's love is for you.

Notice that Paul doesn't pray that you would love God more. He prays that you would grasp his love for you—love that goes beyond your ability to understand. God longs for you to continue every day to take in how much he loves you. And he longs for you to know that love before he ever commands you to live graciously with others.

Do you see how Paul never forgets the gospel? The bridge between entering God's family and learning how to live in it is a regular experience of God's love. As we've already seen, the way we grow in God's family is the same way our smaller families also grow. So as you experience his love and as he lives in you, your conversations will sound more like his. The words you choose, the ways you put them together, and the purposes for which you speak them are all influenced by the present, ongoing relationship you enjoy with him.

Those renewed conversations are vital to the health of God's family and to your own. Since the goal of our conversations is to give grace to those who hear, the next chapter helps us realize that encouragement and honesty are two important, grace-based skills you need to develop to help meet that goal.

18

Speaking Truth and Love

Unloving Truth

Barbed witticisms are delicious. There are several snappy rejoinders attributed to Winston Churchill that, despite being apocryphal, never fail to elicit a laugh because the tables get turned so quickly and decisively on the person initiating the attack.

For instance, one of his bodyguards reported (though some doubt it actually happened) that Bessie Braddock, then a member of Parliament, was appalled at Churchill's condition one time and exclaimed, "Winston, you are drunk, and what's more, you are disgustingly drunk."

To which Churchill replied, "Bessie, my dear, you are ugly, and what's more, you are disgustingly ugly. But tomorrow I shall be sober and you will still be disgustingly ugly."[1]

Now, assuming the account is accurate, these are not people who feel like they just don't know what to say in awkward moments. They do not need to take classes or go to counseling to learn to communicate better. They're actually doing a terrific job at getting their point across. They know exactly what they want

---

1. Richard Langworth, ed., *Churchill by Himself: The Definitive Collection of Quotations* (New York: PublicAffairs, 2008), 550, as referenced by quoteinvestigator. com/2011/08/17/sober-tomorrow/.

to say and are extremely clear in saying it. In that sense, they are good communicators.

But they don't communicate goodness. Their words don't develop a relationship worth having in the moment nor one that they might anticipate enjoying in the future. The words are direct, possibly even accurate, but they're not couched in a framework of care and concern for the other person. In that sense, they are speaking a version of truth, but it's truth without love. While you and I may not be that bold or witty, we've all experienced and participated in this kind of truth-telling that has little regard for the other person.

But God doesn't speak like this. When he speaks truthfully to his people, it is always for the purpose of bringing them closer to himself. He intends his truthful observations and direct conversations to deepen or restore relationships with himself. That's another way of saying that his directness is in the other person's best interest. It is for the sake of the person who is listening.

You've had plenty of experiences where the opposite is true. Has anyone ever said something to you like, "Well, that was a stupid thing to say"? You know what? It very well may have been, but the way the other person communicated that truth to you didn't help you. And that's my point. That person wasn't trying to help and so the "truthfulness" left you feeling foolish, embarrassed, humiliated, resentful, or angry.

When people speak truth that is not aimed at helping you, it's because they have a different agenda than God does. They want to feel clever or superior or less frustrated or in control. And so they speak in ways that mimic truth, but that fall short of real truthfulness because they're not speaking for your good. They may even tell you that they're being "authentic" or "genuine," but if they have no concern for you, then they're authentically and genuinely consumed with themselves.

So how do we describe words that call attention to someone's failings or weaknesses in a way that hurts or embarrasses? Usually we think of them as sarcasm or criticism. In short, it's truth that tears down, which is not really truth.

Untruthful Love

On the other hand, sometimes you can be so concerned for the other person's feelings that you don't say the difficult things he or she needs to hear.

In the 1995 award-winning movie, *Babe*, a young pig is brought to a farm where he develops friendships with many of the other animals. Not one of his new friends, however, tells him what they all know: that in the farm family's mind, pigs are for eating.

Instead, they feel sorry for him as they talk about him behind his back. Eventually he does learn the truth, but the reality hits him so hard at a bad moment that it nearly destroys the one opportunity he has to save his life. Keeping the truth from Babe painted a false picture of reality in his mind that nearly kept him from acting in his own best interests.

That's (obviously) a fictional story, and so little harm is done. Unfortunately, I know stories that aren't fictional. Like the young woman who met a guy she really liked. They started dating seriously, and she was excited. They shared a lot in common. He was kind. Willing to talk. Mature. They had good times together. And she was hooked.

However, he also had a history of failed relationships. Despite his best intentions, he did things that steadily ate away at the foundation of his female friendships. He would start well and end badly. The problem was that she didn't know this about him, and he didn't warn her.

Neither did the other people around her who were well aware of his pattern. She was so happy, no one wanted to say anything. "Why ruin her fun? Besides, who knows, maybe this time will be different." But it wasn't, and she was hurt when everything blew up.

It seemed kinder or at least easier not to say anything, so her friends kept things from her that she really needed to know in order to make good decisions about her life. Their love didn't go very deep. They were unwilling to speak up and tell her hard but important things. Doing so would not have been easy, but it would have been an act of real love and compassion.

Love without truth is not really love. And here's the irony: as different as this sounds from truth-without-love, it's related because it too comes from a heart that is not motivated by the other person's best interest.

If I'm unwilling to speak honestly to you when you need it— if you're in trouble and I won't make the effort to help you see the problem—then I really don't care about you. I care about something else more. It's not simply that I don't want to hurt you or I don't want to make waves, but I want those things more than I want to help.

I want them more than I want to see you built up and strengthened. I want them more than I want to see you protected. I want them more than I want to see you becoming the person the Lord has given his life to produce. When those things control me, then I'm not operating out of real love.

So what do we call communication when someone knows what is true, but won't say it out of fear? Sometimes it's hypocrisy; sometimes it's mealymouthed or wishy-washy sentimentality. And sometimes it even masquerades as tolerance. Regardless, it's a counterfeit of love that keeps the other person from being strong; therefore, it's not really love.

You Need Both to Have Either

When you see that truth without love tears people down and love without truth keeps them weak, then you realize that you cannot really have truth or love unless you have both of them at the same time. That's why Paul insists on combining them in Ephesians 4:15: "Rather, speaking the truth in love, we are to grow up in every way into him who is the head, into Christ."

As children in God's family, we grow and mature through the simple activity of talking to each other, but only when our conversations combine truth and love. And that's a combination that's really hard to achieve.

If you're anything like me and my friends, it's much easier to fall off on one side or the other than to incorporate the two. That means we all have something to work on regardless of how long we've known the Lord or how good our relationships are. Some of us will need to work at being more truthful while others will need to develop greater compassion when we speak.

If you find yourself typically using truth to tear down and you want to see your conversations with your kids mature, then you'll need to practice speaking truth that builds up. One way of thinking about this is that you want to grow in your ability to *encourage* others—to speak love-infused truth. You want to become better at seeing the good that is true of someone else and calling it out to urge them along.

On the other hand, if you find yourself more typically holding back your words in a way that keeps others weak, then you'll need to practice love that speaks up. You want to grow in being able to speak *honestly* with others for their sake—to speak truth-rich love. You want to learn to call people's attention to things in themselves or in their lives that could really hurt them if not addressed.

In the next section, we'll start by thinking about what it means to be an encourager.

Part 3

THE SKILL OF
ENCOURAGEMENT

Speak truth that builds others up.

19

When Should You Encourage?

I once counseled a man who needed to figure out how to talk to his wife. She had come across their daughter's journal earlier that day and read it. As teens are wont to do, the daughter had not been careful in how she talked about her mother or the other things she was doing or thinking that were upsetting.

In the past, something like this would have set the mother off, taking out her hurt on the child with a blistering outburst: "You don't love us. We work and work to care for you, and this is the kind of thanks we get. You should just get out."

This time, however, the mother did not attack. She held her tongue. More than that, she stayed engaged with the needs of the family—helping with homework and making dinner for everyone while she waited for her husband to come home so she could get his thoughts on what to do with what she found. This was real growth for her, and yet, her husband was still concerned about what his wife had done. You see, they disagreed on whether reading a child's diary is okay or not. Obviously, his wife didn't have a problem with this, but he did.

Previously, they had told their kids that one good way to work through their feelings is to write them down. That way the kids can learn what they're feeling and start figuring out how to handle it. The husband believed that if Mom and Dad took what the kids wrote and threw it back in their faces, then they would be punishing their kids for doing what they had been told.

Do you see how tangled life is normally? I'm sure this happens in your home every day. It does in mine. You're regularly handed situations in which you see a mix of both good and bad. The husband is truly grateful for the way his wife is growing. She fought against her pattern of flipping out on the kids that would have generated another relational crisis between them and her. That would have been so easy for her to do given how deeply she was hurt by what she read. But she controlled her reaction in order to serve her family and to ask for help before attempting to deal with the situation.

And yet . . . if she had never read the journal in the first place, then this would not have been an issue. Especially since what she read was four to five months old and didn't reflect how her relationship with the daughter had been steadily improving over the previous months. It's confusing for the husband to sort out what he should pay attention to and what he should say.

So I asked him if we could back up for a moment to get a bigger picture of what was happening. I said, "It seems to me that lots of situations are like this. They come with elements that are really good as well as things that we think are wrong. Life hands you these tangled knots, and then you have to say something that's going to call attention to some of the elements and not to others. So, how do you figure out which ones to focus on?

"Jesus confronts and rebukes many times in Scripture. He points out the misshapen pieces, calls them evil, and directs the person to give them up. Can you think of the kinds of people that he typically does this with?"

As the husband and I pondered that question, we realized that Jesus typically reserves his harshest rebukes for the Pharisees, for hypocrites who are stubbornly set on seeing themselves as righteous, for people who refuse to see.

On the other hand, the apostle Paul opens his first letter to the Christians living in Corinth by lavishing praise on them. He calls them saints (1 Cor. 1:2). He gives thanks for them because of the grace of God that was given to them (1:4). He talks about how they've been enriched in their speech and knowledge such that they're not lacking any spiritual gift (1:7). If he ended his book there, you'd be tempted to think these are wonderful people that you'd love to invite over for dinner.

But then you read the rest of the book and discover they're a mess. They have divisions and rivalries among them that have splintered the church into several different factions (1 Corinthians 3–4). They've tolerated a kind of sexual immorality that non-Christians wouldn't (chap. 5). They file lawsuits against each other (chap. 6) and can't figure out how to think about food sacrificed to idols (chap. 8). They don't sound like people to whom grace has been given and who are enriched in knowledge. They don't sound like people you should say such encouraging things to, but Paul did.

So back up and ask, "What's the difference between the Pharisees and the Corinthians?" Here's what I see: one group arrogantly refused to listen to godly counsel, while the other—for all their sins and errors—demonstrated a softness in their spirits. In his second letter to them, Paul commends the Corinthian believers for having responded to his earlier letter with humble contrition and repentance (2 Cor. 7:8–13). They were not a hardened group of people, and so Paul had no problem beginning by encouraging them.

I then asked the husband I was counseling: "So what do you see in your wife when she talked with you about the diaries? Hardness or softness?"

And he said, "Honestly, I see softness there. She responded with self-control and continued to love our daughter."

In that case, I want to lead with encouragement. There may be things to correct—Paul certainly did with the Corinthians later on—but he started by pointing out the positives. If in each Christian there is a combination of the sinful nature against which we struggle and the active Holy Spirit at work sanctifying us, then I expect to see evidence of both. And I'll probably see both in the same situation. That means I can be just as effective by encouraging growth in godliness and holiness as I can by confronting and rebuking sin.

Actually, maybe you can be more effective. Christians are in the process of being perfected, until one day, only goodness will remain. You're destined for never-ending, eternal holiness. Sin, however, has a shelf life. God's people only wrestle with it internally during this lifetime, and then it will be gone. So when you engage God's children, where do you want to invest your time and relational energy? Into dealing with something that won't survive the next one hundred years? Or into something that will be robustly alive and well trillions of years from now? I want to get better at urging people to grow into what God has planned for them.

Now obviously this is only true when the other person wants to live rightly. Encouraging a Pharisee simply reinforces his own sense of superiority. And working with someone who has no interest in holiness calls for a different approach. But if you are talking to someone who has at least some interest in godliness and who shows some willingness to hear, then practice becoming an expert at using words that encourage. They're the antidote to criticism and sarcasm.

Encouraging Is Like Coaching Six-Year-Olds

My middle son loved playing baseball, and I got drafted into helping coach his teams. The only problem was that I knew next to nothing about baseball.

When I was around twelve years old, I decided I wanted to play Little League Baseball. That meant I was six or seven years behind everyone else. I was put into a league that was only for twelve-year-olds, but was comprised of kids who already played on other teams and who had been doing so for years. Since I did not have a regular team, I never got any kind of practice, but I showed up for the special League games.

I will never forget my first time up to bat. Standing at the plate I forgot everything that I was supposed to know. I forgot I was supposed to look for batting signs from the coach—not that I would have known what they meant if I had looked for them. I forgot to get out of the catcher's way so that he could throw the ball back to the pitcher—forcing him to gently nudge me aside with his glove . . . each time. I suspect that to everyone in the stands it looked like I forgot to swing . . . each time.

That's what stands out to me from my childhood experience of playing baseball. That, and running hard to field a pop-up only to watch it drop two feet in front of me because I pulled up at the last moment, uncertain as to whether it was mine or the shortstop's . . . who had backed off to let me catch it.

So nearly thirty years later, here I was "coaching" baseball, and they told me, "Go coach first base." I thought to myself, "Okay, this is a good start. I know where first base is."

So I headed out, very self-conscious in my official team shirt—which made me feel like I was committing some kind of fraud every time I put it on—only to discover that "coaching" six-year-olds meant I was essentially a cheerleader:

- I smiled at them as they stepped nervously up to the plate.
- I clapped for them to let them know I was pulling for them when they started to get anxious, and I called out, "Here we go. Here we go. You can do this."
- I told them to calm down as I made a soothing motion with my open hands held out, palms aimed at the ground.
- I cautioned that they should pick their pitch when they swung wildly.
- And when they hit the ball, I yelled like crazy, "Run, run, run! Come on, all the way through. Good job!"

- Then we did our celebratory high-five ritual as they proudly stood on the bag.

And then something amazing happened. They started talking to me. They told me about their experience of batting—what it was like, what they were thinking, how well they hit the ball, or how they were afraid they were going to strike out. And then the conversations would drift:

- They pointed out a friend from school who played on the other team.
- They told me what they were doing earlier that day or where they were going later.
- They let me know they couldn't make the next game because they would be going on vacation and they were really excited.
- I was told about (and shown) cuts or scrapes someone got or what happened to them at school.

What happened between me and these young people? I really didn't know anything about baseball, but these kids knew I loved them and cared about them, because of the way I talked to them and encouraged *them* in what *they* were doing. And from that experience of me, they opened up. They reached back and we built a relationship.

There are skills you can learn and develop to become better at encouraging, but here's the bottom line: it's not rocket science. Encouragement is not beyond you or me, nor is it something that we can afford to think is not that big a deal. It powerfully affects others and dramatically opens up relationships.

20

Encouragement Takes Time

Years ago when I worked for a computer company, one of the engineers boasted about the appliances and furnishings in his house. After extolling how beneficial each one was, he concluded, "I won't have anything in my house that won't pay for itself."

Yes, he was young and full of himself, but I still cringed, wondering how his attitude would affect a future wife or children. You can't create a positive context for relationships by evaluating whether someone is paying you back enough—and you're completely deceived if you think you can live life always looking to get back at least what you spent, and not have that attitude spill over into your relationships.

It was similar to the jarring feeling I had years later when the bumper sticker on a van in front of me crudely declared, "Nobody rides for free," along with several payment options. Clearly the person who crafted the sticker and the one who displayed it felt no qualms about boldly proclaiming that a relationship with them was always going to cost the other person more than it cost them.

Would you want a relationship with any of these people? No? Why not? Because their words have communicated that you're not worth their time unless you bring enough to the table to make up for what you cost. God communicates something totally different: "And I heard a loud voice from the throne saying, 'Behold, the dwelling place of God is with man. He will dwell with them, and they will be his people, and God himself will be with them as their God'" (Rev. 21:3).

A day is coming when God's deepest desire will become reality—his people will all be together, living with him and he with them, forever. He's not satisfied with grabbing a couple of hours with you here and there in some haphazard kind of way. He's arranging for a future with you that stretches far beyond any horizon you can imagine. He wants you. And get this: he doesn't keep that knowledge to himself. He makes sure, with simple words, that you know that he wants to spend not just a little bit of his valuable time, but all of it with you.

Now, who do you think stands to benefit most from that arrangement: you or God? Obviously, you will. If God had to be paid back for what he puts into the relationship, then he couldn't spend eternity with you because you couldn't afford him.

How are you feeling now about your relationship with him? Starting to feel a little more encouraged? A little more built up as a person? If so, it's because he let you know that he wants to be with you.

Our modern world pushes against valuing people. We tend to race around, constantly relating to people, but in ways that are shallow because we're either too busy or too wrapped up in what we want from someone or in what we are trying to get done.

My wife works hard to push against that shallowness by letting me know I'm worth her time. She asks me about me and she really wants to know. A number of years ago, after dinner one night she asked how my day had gone and immediately, on cue, the kids barged in, demanding attention, each wanting something different. I was overwhelmed by the onslaught so I brushed Sally off with my best guy-answer, "Fine. My day was fine."

But "fine" wasn't good enough for her. When we settled the kids, she pursued me by restarting the conversation and asking specifically, "How did your meeting go this morning?" She then left what she was doing in the kitchen, walked over to where I was sitting in the living room, settled herself next to me, and gave me her full attention.

Here was real evidence that my wife cared. She wanted to know and relate to me so badly that she wasn't deterred by the distractions that felt to me like too much trouble to overcome. She was determined to spend time with me. And that's when I did open up, responding to someone who clearly told me I was worth her time. I was encouraged.

I see the same dynamic with our kids. Sometimes they need Sally and me to proactively pursue them, intentionally carving out time for them and communicating through that time that they are special and important. I've come home after thinking about one of them during the day and searched for them until I find him or her. Then I've said something like, "Hey! Do you know what today is?"

Generally that question gets me the side-eye and a wary guess: "Tuesday?"

"No." I roll my eyes then smile, "Today is Danny-day, and all day long I've been thinking about spending time with you tonight. Do you think you might have time to hang out with me?" Then I get a big grin in response and a lot of suggestions about what we could do.

At other times, I've had to be ready to be reactive, to drop what I'm doing for the sake of relating to a person who feels a need to talk in the moment. This is harder for me, but especially important for one of our children.

Tim thinks a lot about his life and experiences, but isn't always ready to share his thoughts. That's especially true when he's just gotten back from an important athletic event or time with friends or a week or weekend away with the youth group. It's never a good idea to press him when he comes in the door, but to wait, because he will circle around and talk. Only you better be ready, because it's all going to come out in one nonstop stream of consciousness, and then afterward, he'll be done and won't be revisiting it.

So no matter when Tim starts or what time it is, I stop what I'm doing and I listen. Sometimes I have to mentally coach myself: "Put down your book. Turn off the TV. Don't grumble. Don't interrupt. Pay attention. This is important." And it always is. It's always worthwhile, and I'm always glad when he includes me in his world.

It seems strange, but those relatively small interactions have big effects. After being appropriately proactive or reactive, we've often seen that our young people seem calmer and more secure because they know—they've been reminded—that they count.

One of my former pastors once said, "Quality time is an accident that comes out of quantity time." In other words, you cannot generate a quality-time experience. It requires not just your participation, but your child's as well, and you can't force it: "Okay, get ready. We're going to have a meaningful interaction starting *now.*" Relationships don't work like that.

You can, however, make quantity time happen. You can loosen up your schedule. No one on their deathbed ever looks back wistfully and regrets not having put in more time at the office or wishing they'd run the vacuum cleaner a few more times. They regret not having carved out time to be with the people around them.

You can make time to engage your children in ways that they would like. Those quantity times create contexts in which meaningful interactions often do take place. If you want to encourage your children, think outside of preplanned, rigidly structured schedules and events. Then invite them. Take time with them . . . or more accurately, let them take your time . . . or even better yet, gift them with the time God has gifted to you.

21

Replace the Negatives at Home and Abroad

Think about what it's like to be around a critical person. Critical people are equal opportunity critics, meaning they can be equally vicious publicly, not just privately, often sharing the things you aren't good at with others.

Enduring private criticism is bad enough, but being criticized publicly is like having someone confess your sins for you, only you never know when, where, with whom, or how many that person is going to confess.

I know. Not because of how badly I've been hurt—although I have had plenty of those experiences as well—but because for years this was a typical way that I related. I criticized other people, making them look bad in the eyes of the person I was talking to so that I ended up looking good by comparison. This went on for decades.

Sadly, this pattern didn't register with me until I slowly started to see how often I talked about my wife's faults—not to guard her or help her, but to make me look better. You can imagine the effect this had on Sally. It's not surprising that she found it hard to believe my friends thought well of her when I was busy running her down.

If criticism is the act of publicizing people's failures and short-comings to them and to others, then one important element of encouraging is learning the art of publicizing their strengths and accomplishments, both to them and to others. This art, like any other, takes dedication and hard work. But it's also an art that rewards you with real growth and development.

Notice What Others Do Well

As with all character change, you first need to commit yourself to a new way of living. It is important that you decide to stop speaking critically, but that alone isn't enough. You can't just stop sinning without simultaneously moving in a positive direction.

Again, thinking about Sally, I realized that since my problem involved tearing her down to others, then part of change meant helping others see how good she is. In other words, I needed to intentionally highlight her strengths when I talked about her; to show her in a good light.

That meant I had to do some hard work—not because she makes it hard to speak well of her, but because I'd trained myself not to. So I had to sit down before I met with other people and think of the ways I'd be tempted to pull out her faults—having a sense of my temptations helped me be more careful not to give in to them. Then I thought carefully about what stories I could tell that displayed her strengths and focused on them.

Can you hear that it takes real work and effort to practice being an encourager in a critical, negative world? That it doesn't just happen?

But what if you sit down and nothing positive comes to mind? What if the only things you can think of are negative? What if you have slipped into a mode where the people around you don't do anything right? What if you walk around with your radar on high alert catching them in everything they're doing wrong?

That happens to me too. Thankfully, there's still hope. When I find myself in that trap, I've learned to remind myself, "This can't be true. People are not one-dimensional—they are more than the sum total of their faults. Even those who don't yet know Christ are still made in the image of God and are not yet as fully corrupt and evil as they might be. That means I can't let myself believe the lie that they only ever do everything wrong. It's time for me to catch them doing things right."

And so I will start wandering around the house, intentionally looking for things that my family is doing well that I can then say something about. Sometimes those things are small like noticing and bringing attention to:

- the child who comes quickly to dinner when she's called
- someone who simply brushes his teeth instead of fussing about it
- a six-year-old who moves something away from her baby brother because it might hurt him
- a kid who agrees with what you've been trying to point out instead of arguing about it
- the young person who does his daily chore—emptying the dishwasher, making his bed, putting his laundry away, cleaning the cat's litter pan, setting the table—without being nagged or reminded

Nothing on that list is earth-shattering. But all are important. When people drive you to distraction by drifting along in a self-absorbed fog for days and weeks on end, then any movement outside of themselves is positive and noteworthy and should be called out. I've made a point to thank others for closing a cabinet door without being asked because they and I both needed me to acknowledge that they were thinking about the good of others in that moment and not just thinking about themselves.

It's not the size of the good that people do that makes it worth encouraging. It's that they've done something—anything!—that pushes against their innate self-obsession that is further fueled by living in a self-absorbed world.

A home that focuses on what people are doing well has a re-freshingly different atmosphere from a home that reinforces that nothing anyone does is ever worthwhile or good enough. Your kids will know you appreciate them and their efforts. They will understand that your eyes are on them for good, not evil. That you don't see them primarily as troublesome and never able to do anything right. That there are things they should value and work hard at developing in themselves. Look for these things and use words to bring them out into the open.

Tell Your Kids What You Like about Them

Here's another relatively easy skill to develop: tell people what you like about them. This is different from simple flattery. Flattery is insincere, and everyone knows it. It aims to puff others up in hopes that you'll get something from them in return. Instead, you want to say things that strengthen your child because those things are true and other people know that you believe it.

One easy entry level is simply talking about things that you like about them. Maybe it's their humor, outgoing personality, compassionate heart for others, clear connection with the Lord, or ability to have serious conversations. Maybe they're good at sports or artistic endeavors, fascinated by science, kind to ani-mals, or good at cooking, baking, building, or cleaning.

Can you remember the last time that you pointed out a characteristic of your child that you like? So often we take these things for granted after we've been around our kids, but it really is important to keep letting them know.

And if you can't think of anything that they're good at, then let this moment be a wake-up call for you. Since each child is made in God's image, each one reflects him and his glory, often in surprising and unique ways. If you're struggling to see how yours does, then ask the Holy Spirit to help you see what God has built into them. Then call attention to it.

My son Timmy rarely gets lost. He has a sixth sense for direction that helps him orient himself in the world so that he knows where he is and where he's going. I don't have that gift, and so one day coming out of the mall I asked him where the car was. Sally thought I was testing him, but I really had no idea.

So I told them how years earlier I discovered that it is possible to locate your car after a Major League Baseball game even if you've misplaced it. You simply wait forty-five minutes or so until it's one of the last few left in the lot then walk around the stadium until you see it sitting by itself off in the distance (that strategy doesn't work as well at the shopping mall in the middle of the day).

I told them that was also the night I crossed the Delaware River three times in a row because somehow, coming off the bridge, I got into a lane that sent me back across the river in the opposite direction to where I just was.

I told my family those stories not to run myself down, but to build Tim up. I wanted us to see his gifts and encourage him in the ways that God has gifted him—to help him see that what comes easily to him is not common to all human beings. But there's more. Look closely enough at Tim, and you see a bit of what God is like. God never gets lost. He always knows where he is as he flawlessly navigates his own universe and knows where he left things.

I see some of God when I see my son, and I like that about Tim. I admire him for it. And that means I need to make sure that I say out loud what I'm already thinking so that he knows what I think and feel.

Build a Family Culture That Affirms Each Other's Strengths

Those times of affirming how someone is special can be spontaneous, but you can also build them into your family culture. I heard something on a ministry program years ago that struck me as doable, so I tried it. It was Sally's birthday that night, and at the dinner table I said that I wanted each person in the family to think about one thing that he or she really liked about Mom and tell her during dinner.

One son burst out, "One thing! Oh man, I can't do just one thing!" and then he started talking about how special her hugs and kisses are when she tucks him in. The other two jumped in, and while I can no longer remember what everyone said, I do remember that each person had something to share and that they were all worth hearing. It was a time to honor her and encourage her by letting her hear the things that we really like and value about her.

And it didn't stop with her. We did the same thing for the next person's birthday and the next and the next until it has become a family tradition. And it's a tradition that everyone takes responsibility for. I was both surprised and really pleased the first time I didn't start the conversation, but one of the kids beat me to it. In that moment, they were owning and practicing a lifestyle of encouragement.

Those are powerful moments that leave you a bit in awe. You're amazed and delighted to hear young people thank you for making dinner or for working on the house or for getting them a new bike or for taking them places. Those are moments that don't happen all the time and you certainly can't live for them, but they really do happen as your kids adopt the tone and pace that you set by learning to encourage them.

The alternative is what one husband experienced with his wife. Whenever he tried to encourage her, she didn't respond positively, but became prickly and agitated. When I asked him if he had any idea why she reacted like that, he traced it back to her childhood experience of living in a family that never said anything encouraging to her.

While "never" is a strong word—and may even have been hyperbolic—the result of her upbringing was that even when someone close to her tried to build her up, she grew suspicious, wondering, "What does he want now?"

Does that mean she doesn't need to be encouraged? No, it means she needs a regular, steady diet of it until her malnourished soul learns to receive it properly. This is one powerful way her husband will continue to love her.

It's the same kind of love your kids need to hear from you.

22

Search for the Positive in Seed Form

You need to encourage people for who they are, and you need to encourage them for who they are becoming. Your children are in process. They are changing, growing, and developing, and they need you to help them do so by urging them in positive directions.

Immaturity doesn't grow up overnight. Patterns don't change quickly. Real change is most often of the small, incremental variety. That means each footstep down a new road is hard won and deserves to be celebrated, not overlooked or taken for granted.

I was counseling a teenage son who was working on building a more open relationship with his parents. He had a history of hiding things he did that he knew they didn't like. One day his mother asked him to take out the trash, and he wasn't exactly quick about it. But when he eventually got around to it, he was convicted of his sloppy attitude toward her and what she wanted from him, so he went back to her and told her he was sorry he hadn't obeyed quickly.

For this young man that was not only different; it was difficult. He voluntarily opened up the inner workings of his heart and mind despite how bad it made him look. I made a big deal about it because I figured, "If he's telling me this, he knows how big a milestone this is for him." Then I wondered out loud if his mom had noticed.

"No," he said with a sheepish half-smile, "I don't think she did."

Here's a place where his mom has to be on the lookout for these small signs of where her son is maturing. These moments happen every day—moments when our children try something that's hard for them. Notice those moments and verbally celebrate them, and your child will see you as an ally, someone who is on their side.

Look for What Your Kids Are Working On

But that means I need to be tuned in to what my children are working on in their lives, and that can be difficult for me. I find that I assume too often that they're not working on anything. Or I get upset because I see them doing a million irritating things that I think they should have corrected long ago. That mind-set isn't helpful as it only serves to supercharge my critical nature.

I find it sobering in those moments to stop and realize that there are still, conservatively speaking, probably several million things that God needs to work out in my life. Oddly enough, he seems to focus me on only one or two of them at a time, and then just for a few weeks, before we move on to the next one.

That means it's vital for your ministry of encouragement to be keyed into looking for what God is doing in the lives of your children. God tells us he is actively at work in everyone's life (Matt. 5:45; Luke 6:35; Rom. 1:19) and especially the lives of his people (Phil. 1:4–6), but sometimes we speak and act like he isn't. That's coming close to accusing God of lying. Look hard. Where do you see him softening your children's consciences? Convicting them of sin? Sanctifying old patterns? Increasing their faith? Maturing them in learning to reach out and help others?

In other words, the process by which someone matures is just as important as the end result because the process leads to the result. So if I'm going to engage my kids like God engages me, I need to zero in on the one or two things that they're working on at any given time.

One Friday evening my wife and I went to a dinner party. These can be difficult for me because left to myself I tend to have solitary habits. I love people, but, being an extreme introvert, I'm not energized by being with people, which means I need time away to recharge. I enjoy working alone in my office with the phone set on voice mail and an assistant guarding the door. And I can be quite happy that way for hours.

So when people invite us out, sometimes I have to fight to go with a good attitude because most of the time I prefer staying home. So why go? It tends to be some mixture of (1) my wife, who is not an introvert, is energized by being with people, (2) our friends are blessed by being with us, and (3) deep down I know and agree with God's assessment that it's not good for humans to be alone (Gen. 2:18).

So we went to the party, and on the way home Sally leans over in the car and says, "You did really well. You talked to people, didn't hide, and were fun. No one there would have known how hard that was for you."

That was really special. Her words, unlooked for, broke into my world. They told me that she understands me and cares about how I experience life and that she's watching out for me. She sees what I'm working on, gets that it's not easy, and puts her awareness and care into words to urge me to keep going. If I need that, how much more do our kids?

Focus on Why Your Kids Do What They Do

But what if you don't know what someone is trying to do differently? One easy way is simply to ask. It's humbling, but numerous times I've had to go to my kids when I'm frustrated by all that I think they're not doing and ask them to tell me what it is that they are focusing on because I just don't know.

One word of caution: when you do that, you need to be careful, because it's easy to let frustration give your question an edginess that makes it sound like one more criticism—akin to, "Are you doing *anything*?" I've noticed, however, that when I ask it honestly, the question itself draws us closer because they realize that I'm more interested in their lives than in how they're affecting me.

But what if your children can't relate to the question because they're more reactive than proactive? What if they don't think in terms of goals and change because they're more scared and retiring than outgoing and initiating? You can still find ways to encourage them to grow. Listen to their fears and weaknesses, then look for moments when they take even timid steps to push against those things. Again, remember, you're looking to encourage them in the process of growth, not just looking for completely developed maturity.

Or you might be thinking, "But I don't see anything that they're doing that I can fully support. Everything they do still has elements that need to be corrected." That's probably true of my life as well, and yet, if you look below the surface of what I actually do, often you can discern a motive that's at least moving in the right direction. Try that with your children. Try looking past what they've done to why they did it, and see if there's at least a desire to do what is good and right.

Cassie and I went shopping together when she was around six years old. When we got back home, she went into the house in front of me, raced up the stairs, and then slammed the door shut in my face as I was trying to carry several bags into the house. I was tempted to berate her for being inconsiderate, but I had been thinking earlier that day about learning to speak well to my family. So, trying not to sound frustrated, I decided to ask, "Hey, can you help me understand why you did that?"

She responded, "So that Danny [her baby brother who was crawling all over the house] didn't fall down the stairs."

Ok, here's an example where I would have chosen to act differently, but clearly she was motivated by something that I could support. I would have lost that chance to think well of my daughter, however, if I didn't look below the surface of what she did and ask why she did it. If you're not used to looking for motives, take heart. This is something you can learn.

It's also something your kids can learn.

Sally was making gravy one night to go with the chicken she baked, and our youngest decided to volunteer his culinary opinion by telling her, "That looks yucky."

Before Sally could respond, our elementary-aged middle son jumped in and said to Danny, "Can you learn to say, 'Thank you for making dinner even if I don't like it,' because you need to be thankful to the person who's making your food?"

Danny paused, digested this new perspective, then spoke up again: "That sauce looks yucky, but I'm just going to eat it."

And I thought, "Fantastic! I have something to encourage in both of them because they're both trying really hard." I said, "Danny, I see your heart in trying to be thankful for dinner, and Timmy, I see a young man who is working hard to help his younger brother. Thank you. You've both done really well."

Timmy was helping his brother learn how to be thankful in an age-appropriate way. Danny was trying hard to appreciate his mother. Granted, neither said things exactly the way I would have, but both were working hard, and I could appreciate their desire.

Not only should I appreciate my children's steps toward growth, but I can and must encourage them. It's too easy to focus on the goal and ignore the process by which someone is moving toward it. Learn to see the process with its countless steps and stages and you'll quickly see many things you can encourage.

23

Be Encouraged When You're Tired of Encouraging

Encouraging is necessary work, but sometimes it feels like too much work. At least Sandra thought so. She had had it. Weeks of potty training Corey with nothing to show for it—literally. She'd done it all: doled out M&M incentives, bought cool potty pants, made potty charts with stickers, taught the potty dance, set out books alongside the potty, and even offered a special gift for repeated success. Nothing worked.

One day they were in the mall, of all places, and Corey said, "I have to go potty." But by this time Sandra was all done. She looked at Corey and told her, "You have a diaper on; use it," as she thought, "I am not taking you to a public restroom to watch you do nothing."

Ever been there? We all have. Your child may not have run you past your limit with potty training, but he surely has with something else. We've all had times where we've worked and worked, encouraging and urging our children to handle the challenge in front of them, and they refused to do or even try doing anything different. They wouldn't play with the other kids in the neighborhood, start their homework before launching a computer game, make their bed, clean up their room, finish their dinner, stop swearing, or do something other than gaze lovingly at their phone.

But then there's that moment when things come together for them, and they take a small, tentative step in the right direction. You know you should wildly cheer them on, but you can't. You won't. You're fed up and past being willing to see them do anything right. You have a sense of how difficult it is for them. You might even be able to put it into words, but you just don't want to. You're too angry over everything they've not been doing, and you're unwilling to encourage them. Instead, you're ready to quit.

Have you ever felt like that? Like maybe if they had tried a little earlier, you might have responded decently, but at this point it's just too late? I have.

That's a common dynamic in relationships. One person works hard for a while to engage the other one. People often start out willing enough, but after a while, if there's little to show for all the time and energy they're pouring out, they start to feel drained. They get tired of being affected by the other person's problems, and they start wondering, "Why bother? This isn't going anywhere." So they quit, often at about the same time when the other person wakes up and starts to respond.

Moments like these call for endurance and perseverance, two character qualities that are the hallmark of God's people (see 2 Cor. 6:4; 12:12; 2 Tim. 3:10–11; Rev. 2:2–3). Given how hard it is to live on this planet, it makes sense that we need to be urged, "Don't quit. Don't give up. Keep enduring and persevering" (see 1 Tim. 4:16; Titus 2:2; Heb. 10:36; Rev. 13:10). You will need these two traits if you're going to keep investing in your children by trying to encourage them.

And yet, even though I can see how important these traits are, when I'm worn out by my kids, I don't want to endure or persevere with them. I don't want to try to encourage them anymore. I'm all done.

In those moments I need more than someone telling me, "Buck up. Get back in there and try again." That won't help me want to get back in there. Nor will platitudes that cheerfully try to predict the future: "Don't quit now. You never know—third time's the charm!" And I really don't need someone to make it easier for me to quit: "It's okay. Give it a rest. Maybe you'll feel like trying again later."

When I'm ready to quit, or after I already have, I need more than someone entering into my world to tell me what to do or to tell me what I want to hear. Instead:

- I need someone who will do with me what I am refusing to do with someone else—endure with me when I reject God's good plans for my relationships, and
- I need someone who can get at the control center of my life and adjust it so that I want to endure with others.

In other words, I need the God of Romans 15:5—the God who gives endurance and encouragement. Are you surprised to hear that the source of these two traits is in God before they can ever be in you? Remember, God never calls you to do something that you haven't first experienced. In order for you to endure, you need to know what it's like to be endured with. In order to encourage, you need to know what encouragement sounds like. This God works to give you both endurance and encouragement so that you can pass along that same experience to others.

That means I need to accept that I am needy, that I need to be encouraged. And I need to believe that he longs to encourage me, to meet my need. So I listen to him. I listen to hear his words that tell me he's not given up hope for me (Isa. 40:28–31; Phil. 1:6), that he really does understand how hard life can be on this planet (Heb. 2:17–18; 4:15), and that he will never stop working in me until I am pure and complete, not lacking anything (Heb. 12:2; James 1:2–4; 1 Pet. 2:2). I need to be encouraged by God himself when I see how ready I am to give up.

And I need a God who can put his kind of endurance into me. It's embarrassing to admit that I've received mercy and kindness from him for decades, and yet, I can so easily refuse to extend that same kindness to a fellow struggler. Even then, he hangs in there with me. He endures with me. Now if he could somehow put that same kind of willingness to endure inside me, I would live so much better with the difficult people in my life.

And that's what he does. He gives endurance (Rom. 15:5). He fills you with the knowledge of his will so that it results in "all endurance and patience with joy" (Col. 1:11). And when you're tempted to quit and give up on your kids, you can be certain that he provides a way for you to escape that temptation so that you can endure and be willing to try again (1 Cor. 10:13). Without an active God working in you, you cannot develop endurance like his.

Here's where religiosity and good ideas will fail every time. They don't have life or power in them to change you. At best they can point the way, but without experiencing an active, present relationship with the God who made you, you cannot hope to develop a godly relationship with your child.

There is no deep mystery here of how this happens. When you feel like throwing up your hands, walking out, and giving up, you take words back to your God and talk with him about it. You admit to him that you don't want to do what he's called you to, and you realize that you're now just as difficult and obstinate as your child. You ask him to endure with you by forgiving you. You ask him to encourage you by letting you know that he's not fed up and ready to walk away from you. And then you ask him to put that same kind of enduring, encouraging spirit into you, so that you can go back and reengage your child like he just did with you.

You need to hear encouragement. God hangs in there with you and very willingly speaks to you to keep you from giving up in frustration. The people around you need that same enduring, encouraging experience from him. They'll develop a taste for it as they experience you coming back to them, renewed by a God who does not grow tired of refreshing his people.

Part 4

THE SKILL OF HONESTY

Speak courageously to make others strong.

24

The Goal of Honesty: Rescue

Some of us need to become experts at encouraging our children. Others, however, need to learn to speak more openly and honestly to them when they're in trouble. We're now considering the kind of communication the Bible describes when it uses words like *confront*, *correct*, *rebuke*, or *reprove*.

Let's acknowledge up front that this is a hard topic for many of us. If you're not good at frank, open candor, then those words might make you nervous or even physically ill. It's not easy to think about stepping into someone else's world to challenge what he or she is thinking or doing.

But these words are hard not only for shy, retiring people. I can't recall having met anyone—even someone who has no trouble speaking his mind—who was pining away with a deep longing for someone else to speak as bluntly and directly to him as he enjoyed speaking to others.

What makes courageous truth so unappealing to both the speaker and the hearer? Maybe it has to do with how little we've experienced it. Or maybe it has to do with the many times we've experienced its opposite—times when we've been on the receiving end of confrontations that were not designed to help us, but were for another person's benefit. Times when:

- they were fed up and wanted to get something off their chest
- they wanted you to feel so badly about something, that you would never think to do it again
- they used volume and threats to bully or intimidate or keep you safely at arm's length
- they shredded your self-worth with cold, belittling comments that cut way too close to home

There just wasn't a sense of the other person being for you or wanting to help you. Such past experiences make it hard to talk about confrontation in a way that has a shot at being positive.

Maybe this story will help; but first, you'll need a little background. If someone in my family calls you a bossy moo-cow or for no apparent reason starts making lowing noises, then he or she is quietly suggesting you're overstepping your bounds and are being controlling.

One morning, I was sitting on the couch with my four-year-old daughter. We had just visited with some of her cousins and were talking about the time together. She referred to one of them as a bossy moo-cow. This was amusing to me as Cassie is the one in our family who loves us and has a wonderful plan for our lives.

So, hoping that this was one of those fabled "teachable moments" I asked very lightly, "Yeah, that's true. Um. Do you ever see any of that in you?"

To which she quickly replied, "Oh, no."

And because I am who I am, I stubbornly persisted: "Not even a little bit?"

And because she's my daughter, she also persisted: "No, not even a little."

I figured, *Thus endeth the teachable moment . . .* except my daughter and I live in a sovereign God's universe. At that moment, my two-year-old son wandered into the room pushing a cart. Without skipping a beat, Cass pointed to where we normally keep it and ordered, "Timmy, put that over there."

I exploded off the couch with my arms stretched out wide above my head and cried, "Whoa! Did you see that? This huge cow just came galloping through the room! It had eight-feet-wide horns that touched the ceiling! That was amazing!" I went on and on and on. And my daughter sat on the couch, wide-eyed, laughing. Actually, we laughed together, and then talked about what she'd just done.

Now, is that confrontation?

Of course it is. I'm pointing out something that needs to change. But it's not scary. She's not running from me, either physically or emotionally. Instead, she's interacting with me. I was lighthearted, but she got the point. What is it that made that experience different from the nightmare scenarios we've all experienced? She knew my excessive emotion and volume were not for my sake, but for hers.

Or think about another time several years later, when close friends and relatives firmly shattered the peace of my family in a moment of well-intentioned thoughtlessness. They began giving my daughter Barbie dolls.

She rarely played with them, but she would spend hours dreaming about them. Those tiny accessories, little shoes, and different outfits captivated her. She would turn them around in her mind and envision imaginary Barbie-lands that mattered more to her in the moment than the real world—it was not very different from watching a teenage boy caught up in a video game. Her eyes would glaze over. She'd retreat to that faraway place, and it was like the rest of us no longer existed.

We were having one of those times. She had been flipping through toy catalogs, impassioned by the latest styles and accessories, deeply lost in Barbie lust.

I knew I needed to talk with her about it so I had thought carefully the night before about what to say. I sat down with her the next morning before going to work, and we talked about what I was seeing and the effects that it seemed to be having on her and on us. And then I said, tentatively, "It, um, looks like you love Barbies too much again, huh?"

She nodded, looking at the ground, and said, "Yeah . . . and you love tools too much, Daddy." Both of us burst out laughing because she nailed me.

I can so easily do with tools what she did with Barbies. I find myself in home improvement stores, walking up and down the aisles gazing lovingly at all the power tools. I start talking myself into purchases by imagining all the projects I could do if only I had a fifteen-amp circular saw because, as everyone knows, my thirteen-amp just isn't powerful enough. Plus, I don't have enough yellow tools, and I really need to have one more yellow tool because *everybody* knows that yellow tools are so much better and . . . yeah, Cassie was right. I love tools too much.

We laughed some more, and then I reminded her of how God had worked in her life and mine in the past. We took time to pray together for each other that we would not love God's creation more than we love him. It was a time that underlined how our mutual need of help made us peers at the foot of the cross.

In other words, there is a way to confront that draws people together rather than driving them apart. It's a way that mirrors what God is doing when he speaks honestly. It can be scary to think about God rebuking people in general. It's really frightening to think about him confronting you personally. But look past what he says to why he says it. What is he hoping for when he confronts?

He's hoping that you'll listen and agree with what he sees. He's longing for you to stop going in the same direction and turn away from what you've been doing. Why does he want that for you? So that life will actually be better for you. So that you won't hurt yourself, and so that you'll draw closer to him and to others.

In other words, God doesn't confront to break relationships. He speaks honestly to restore them. That's different from the way many people think about confrontation. We often envision people as being somewhat close before a rebuke, but who might be driven apart if one of them confronts the other. And because we don't want to put any more distance between ourselves and someone else, we pull up short and don't say what needs to be said.

God knows something different. He knows that distance is already there. You're already estranged. Therefore, when he confronts, it is for the purpose of getting rid of the thing that's keeping everyone apart so that they can all be together again. His goals are that by hearing him, you won't harm yourself, that you won't harm others, and that you won't damage his glory. All those things work together at the same time.

So if you're speaking honestly into someone's life like God speaks into yours, then you're trying to keep him from ruining his life. You're trying to rescue him. Or as James puts it at the end of his letter: "My brothers, if anyone among you wanders from the truth and someone brings him back, let him know that whoever brings back a sinner from his wandering will save his soul from death and will cover a multitude of sins" (James 5:19–20).

At its most basic, speaking honestly—going after someone with words to bring that person back—is simply a rescue mission. It's you seeing someone in danger and pursuing him so that he doesn't ruin and destroy himself. Who will most benefit from that interaction? It's not you. It's the other person. When that other-centered motivation drives you, you will find a way to communicate to someone else something along the lines of, "Please hear me so that you don't end up hurting you, and so that you are better off."

25

Think Before You Speak

The goal of godly confrontation is to offer help and healing. You'd never learn that by listening to our society. Instead, confrontation is an attack—a verbal joust aimed at destroying your opponent's argument by any means necessary or, failing that, an attempt to demean your opponent, hoping that will discredit his beliefs.

The memorable sound bite. The acidic quip. The sly innuendo. The spontaneous insult. The unstoppable torrent of words. These are the prized weapons in an assault. The faster, the sharper, the harsher, the better. Glib repartee and sheer wordiness score more points over quieter, carefully reasoned approaches.

At least, they do until you start to listen to wisdom. Wisdom is essential to life. With wisdom you'll thrive, and without it you'll wither. Wisdom lets you align your ways, including your words, with the way that God has set up and organized his world. Line up with him, and you'll live well. Run counter to his ways in his world, and your life will be a never-ending source of frustration and harm to yourself and everyone around you.

You can tell a lot about a person's wisdom based on how he or she communicates. Wisdom has real content, but it also has its own form and style, meaning that you can recognize it when you hear it.

In the book of Proverbs you're introduced to two different people—the person who is wise and the one who is a fool—and you're given lists of characteristics that help you tell the two apart. Wise people are measured in what they say. They weigh their words carefully (Prov. 15:28). They are in control of what comes out of their mouths (Prov. 12:23). They are intentional when they speak (Prov. 16:23). They are thoughtful, considering the potential future impact of what they're saying (Prov. 16:21).

In other words, they take time to think about things (Prov. 14:8). They do have a response in conversations, yet are willing to mull it over and reconsider it before letting it air live. They don't say the first thing that pops into their heads or let their mouths run away with them (Prov. 10:19). As a result, their words benefit others, both helping and healing those who listen (Prov. 10:11, 21; 12:18; 16:21).

Foolish people, on the other hand, shoot their mouths off. They react out loud, immediately and impulsively. They blurt, gush, and speak recklessly in their haste to say what's on their mind, chattering on endlessly (Prov. 12:18, 23; 15:2; 29:20). They give quick, off-the-cuff, speedy responses without taking the time to consider what they're saying or the effect it will have.

Not surprisingly, they damage others, which is often their intent in a war of words (Prov. 12:18). What is surprising is that their words rebound, bringing greater harm to themselves (Prov. 10:11, 14; 18:6). Even though, initially, verbally subduing someone else looks like a power move, eventually it backfires, entangling the fool in even greater problems (Prov. 18:7).

You might struggle to accept Proverbs' description and assessment of how the fool talks, especially if you've been trained to believe that quick, snappy responses and put-downs are best. In our world, someone who stops to think appears slow-witted, and therefore, by definition is already losing the debate.

Proverbs disagrees. It argues that on this side of heaven, what comes quickly, effortlessly, spontaneously, and loudly is foolishness. Wisdom takes time. That's important to remember when you're upset or angry or in the middle of a confrontation. Your first instincts may not be your best. Mine usually are not. My son Tim and I were watching Olympic ice dancing after dinner one evening. When one team was judged to be average, Tim said, "I feel like they should have gotten a higher score." Immediately I bristled. "How can you say that? I don't even know what the scale is, what those numbers mean, how the level of difficulty factors in, or even what to watch for that they're being judged on."

Tim didn't know either. He's a soccer player, a runner, a hurdler, and he has wrestled. On any of those sports he could speak with some authority. But ice dancing? At best he's a casual spectator, catching a couple hours of it every four years. Technically I was right—he had no basis for what he said—but mostly I was foolish.

I was not careful in what I said. I did not stop to think. I instinctively blurted out the first thought that occurred to me. Worst of all, I didn't consider the effect it would have on him. I shut him down, driving him into himself. By mocking him I broke our relationship; understandably, he left the room.

That's when I took some time to think. As I sat there, I realized, "He liked them. He enjoyed watching them, was hoping they would do well, and was disappointed when they didn't. He wasn't thoughtlessly critiquing the judges. It's just the way he expresses himself."

Insight doesn't come quickly in a world plagued by foolishness. It takes time. It also takes the willingness to look at least as critically at yourself as you do at others. Regardless of whether I correctly understood Tim or not, the truth about me was pretty plain. And pretty ugly. I had played the fool, and I was wrong.

That meant I had to take a moment to think even more carefully about what to say next—not to manipulate my son or to try maneuvering him, but to make clear how I had sinned against him and what I was hoping for now. Once it was clear in my own mind, I went looking for him and apologized for speaking harshly and for not making room for him to express himself in his own ways without getting smacked down. And I asked him to forgive me. Thankfully, he did, and we experienced the healing that comes with wisdom.

How Does Jesus Want to Use This Moment?

In order to speak constructively you have to pause long enough to ask, "How does Jesus want to use what I'm about to say to bring his good purposes into this situation?" Regardless of how bad the problem is or how many times it's taken place, every single horrible thing in the believer's life can be reclaimed beyond your wildest imagination. Now that Jesus has risen from the dead, nothing, absolutely nothing, must remain as it is.

That's true *and* I struggle to believe it. Too often I still live pessimistically, believing that the people around me will never be any different, so why bother speaking up? When you live that way, you deny the gospel. You assume that Jesus is not involved and has no interest in being involved. That's not true. And so in times of trouble, I first have to speak to myself, reminding myself that Jesus is at work in the world to bring about good for his children. That means he's working hard to bring good into my family.

Throwing up my hands and walking away from situations I don't like is no longer an option. Nor am I allowed to attempt through anger, bullying, or manipulating to get what I want. Instead, I have to enter situations and look for what Jesus might be up to before I open my mouth. Only after I understand what he's doing can I afford to get involved.

You might be thinking, "That's unrealistic. If I lived like that, I would never get anything done." I'm not talking about some painstaking, arduous activity that will take several hours. Those times do happen, but they tend to be rare. I am talking, however, about doing something that doesn't come immediately, something that requires you to make room for it.

I remember the time one of my children blatantly disobeyed me, literally putting one of their siblings in real, physical danger.

I was furious and knew I wasn't thinking clearly. So I sat the child down on a couch and said, "I don't trust myself to do good to you right now, so I need to go pray before I say or do anything." Then I went into my bedroom and prayed. But instead of calming down, I kept churning inside, mentally racing through all the different things I could do that would really make an impression on my child. None of them, however, seemed quite right, and all left me feeling unsettled.

That's when I realized I was praying for the wrong thing. I wasn't looking for how Jesus wanted to bring about good in the situation; I was just looking for the right, dramatic punishment to make sure something like this never happened again.

It made sense why I wasn't getting an answer. I was praying for something that wasn't on Christ's agenda. So I changed my focus. I started praying to see this as an opportunity for God to break through and use it to bring about his kingdom in the life of my child and my family.

It was surprising how quickly I had a sense of how to speak to this child, along with an idea of what discipline was appropriate within what God wanted to do. It was a very serious time, but I didn't make it worse. Instead we experienced God's restoring desires in the middle of it.

Sometimes it's enough to quietly pursue wisdom on your own with the Lord. Other times you need help. Sometimes I don't trust myself to figure out what redemption looks like, so I keep a short list of go-to people—my wife, a few good friends, and leaders at church—that I can reach out to for advice.

Wisdom teaches that you need to think through what it might sound like to "speak the very words of God" (1 Pet. 4:11 NIV) before you confront. You might not always know. You might need time to pray or to ask your friends. Take that time. Don't be afraid to slow down so you can focus yourself in a more godly direction. Doing anything else is just plain foolish.

26

Be a Mirror That Invites Participation

When I think of what loving honesty looks like, I find it helpful to picture being a mirror to someone else. What does a mirror do? It merely reflects back what is already there. It doesn't create what you see. It doesn't explain what you see. It doesn't predict what you're going to see. It simply shows you in that moment what everyone else already sees. What you do with what you see is then up to you.

In a human interaction, my goal in being a mirror is to say, "Hold up. This is what I see right now as I experience living with you. Take a moment so you can look too. Do you see the same thing or am I missing something?"

A number of years ago my family was having one of those dinners that make you thankful the neighbors can't see through your curtains. It started chaotically and spiraled down from there. Sal and I tried to intervene and redirect the kids who weren't terribly interested in being redirected. Instead of working with us, they started withdrawing sullenly into themselves. I handled their bad response badly, becoming less patient, more critical, and louder by the minute. As I ramped up, the kids shut down even more, staring pointedly at the table and gulping down their food so they could leave the room more quickly.

As much as I struggle with living in the middle of crazy, I struggle even more with being ignored. So in frustration, to no one in particular, I demanded, "Why doesn't anyone answer me when I'm talking to them?"

To which my very brave and kind wife, looked up from spooning food into the baby and said, "Because you're scary when you look like that."

That's not really the answer to the question I thought I was asking, but it was the answer I needed to hear. She was kind and gracious and to the point: "Here is what it is like to live with you. This is how you affect us." She was a mirror.

I need that. Sin is a restless, evil thing. It deceives and hardens you (Heb. 3:12–13). It turns you against your God, and it fools you as it ruins your life. Notice that my wife and kids are not deceived about how scary I look. I am. I am the one who is deceived—tricked, fooled—which means that I am the one who needs help. In such moments I truly believe that I see things the way they are when I don't. I need help. I need a mirror.

And that's what my children need when they're deceived. Being a mirror to them is an essential part of loving them.

In our home we have guidelines for how long people can use electronics in a given day—guidelines that people regularly ignore . . . er, "forget." So I will often find myself telling someone that he or she is over the screen-time allotment on the family computer. Now, what do you do or say when you've reminded your children they're past their limit, but later discover that they're still on?

You could throw the thing out and then you wouldn't have to deal with it again—only, they will once they leave your home and purchase their own. All you'll have done is leave them to wrestle (or not wrestle) with their lack of self-control on their own. Or, you could take away their screen privileges for anything other than homework. It's a less draconian strategy, but it has the same inability to teach them to curb their out-of-control desires as getting rid of the thing. In other words, neither option lets you address their heart, and neither option has a chance of helping them see. And I so badly want them to see.

That means I have found myself going back to them when they are still logged on to a game even after I've told them "Time's up." I say something like, "So . . . when we talked twenty minutes ago and I said, 'You need to get off the computer' you decided to say to me, 'Forget it, Dad. I choose what to do in your house with your computer because I am big enough and I have the right to make those decisions.'"

Now obviously, the child didn't say that out loud, so what am I trying to do? I'm trying to give them a sense of the words and tone that match their actions rather than let them deceive themselves into thinking that "forgetting" is relatively harmless.

Then I pause and invite my child to look a little deeper into the mirror. "Please understand, God put me in your life so that you could learn to live within the borders of someone else's authority. That means you're not going to treat anyone else in authority, including him, with any better respect than you practice with me.

"I'm not trying to make you feel guilty, but to let you see yourself and decide if this is who you want to be. You are going to turn the computer off now, but what you do next is up to you. You can be grumpy and upset. You can think to yourself that this is so unfair. Or, maybe it would be worth spending some time thinking about the kind of person you're turning yourself into. You still have a Savior you can run to who will gladly make you like himself if you don't like seeing what you're becoming."

As long as sin is a present reality for us—tempting us and trying to deceive us—we'll all continue to battle with spiritual blindness. Part of God's solution to that problem is that we become mirrors in each other's lives.

Invite Your Kids to Help Solve the Problem That You See

Sometimes being a mirror ends with saying to someone, "This is what I see . . . what are you going to do with it?" Other times, you can take the additional step of inviting someone's cooperation to resolve the problem that you see. I've found it helpful to think in terms of a simple formula that I learned years ago from a mentor that goes like this:

- When you do or say _____,
- I feel _____, (or I do _____, or I say _____, or I think _____).
- Please help (because I want something better for us, but I can't solve our problems without you).

Notice that just like a mirror, you're not telling someone why he's doing what he's doing. Instead, you're simply describing what you see or experience. You're also not accusing the other person of making you respond in a certain way. You're confessing your tendency to respond in certain ways when other people do or say certain things. Then lastly, you're inviting another person to work with you to resolve the relational strain that is occurring.

Our family found this approach helpful when we were learning to make room for others to talk and share around the dinner table. The kids were still in elementary school and were adopting the dining etiquette of their cafeteria, where everyone talks at once and only the loudest person can be heard.

One evening, after everyone had food in front of them, I asked for their attention and said: "I'm noticing a problem. We all keep interrupting each other and talking over each other so that it's hard to hear what anyone's saying. If we keep doing this, then someone will keep hogging all the airtime and the rest of us will quit trying. So what do you think we should do about it?"

Did you see the three elements?

- Here's what I see: we're all interrupting each other.
- Here's the effect it's having: we can't all share our lives.
- Please help: what do you think we should do about it?

I had no idea what to expect, but I was really surprised. Some ideas weren't really workable, but together we came up with one that was. We decided to make a small pile of "Interruption Tickets" and put them in a basket.

During dinner, anyone could hand you a ticket at any time if you started talking while someone else already was. If you got three tickets during a meal, you lost your speaking privileges for the remainder of the meal. There was no appeal process: you interrupt, you get ticketed. It was a lighthearted way for us to gently confront each other that we invited from each other—the kids *loved* it when one of them handed me a ticket.

The novelty of using the tickets wore off in about a week, but it helped us continue to build a culture in our home that values each person's contribution by intentionally making space for everyone to share what's on their mind.

As helpful as I've found these kinds of tools, please remember, they're only tools. Being a mirror to someone won't change his heart. Even inviting him to participate in solving the problem that you see won't change his heart. Only Jesus changes hearts. These approaches can help your child see where change needs to happen, but you're still relying on Christ to produce the life in them that you long for them to have (John 3:5–8).

27

Aim for the Heart

Pharisees: "Teacher, we know that you are true and teach the way of God truthfully, and you do not care about anyone's opinion, for you are not swayed by appearances. Tell us, then, what you think. Is it lawful to pay taxes to Caesar, or not?"

Jesus: "Why put me to the test, you hypocrites?" (Matt. 22:16–18)

Well. That was abrupt. Think about what it would have been like to hear this interaction. The Pharisees, the morally good church-people, approach Jesus with deference and respect. And Jesus sounds harsh by comparison.

More than that, it seems like he misses the point of the conversation. They're asking about one thing, and he's talking about something totally different; they're trying to discuss an ethical dilemma involving taxes but he's focusing on hypocrisy.

The only reason this exchange makes any sense is because you've already been given insider information that the Pharisees were laying plans to trap Jesus (Matt. 22:15). Their words sounded sweet, but their intent was anything but. Jesus saw through their words and addressed the underlying issue. This was not the first time he did that.

His friend Martha tried to trap him when she was rushing around to provide for a houseful of guests while her sister Mary sat with the guys listening to Jesus. "Lord," she blurted, "do you not care that my sister has left me to serve alone?" (Luke 10:40).

Do you see how she set him up? How's Jesus supposed to answer that question? "No, Martha, I really don't care. Just keep working and leave me out of it"? Or he could get co-opted by Martha's agenda: "Yes, I do care, so Mary, get up and get in line with what your sister wants." There seems to be no good way for him to respond.

Jesus, however, instead of letting himself be maneuvered by an unfair question, transcended the question by addressing Martha's overpreoccupation that had led her to be worried and upset by many things (Luke 10:41).

Another time, a man confronted Jesus: "Teacher, tell my brother to divide the inheritance with me" (Luke 12:13). If Jesus were to stay at the level of the man's words, then he would either have to say, "No, I won't. He can keep it all" or, "Yes, you can use me to be the stick that beats your brother into shape."

Jesus again went below the surface conversation to have a more important one. He told a story that identified the greed that controlled both brothers, and in targeting that issue, invited them both to repent or be judged (Luke 12:14–21).

In other words, Jesus didn't always respond to people's literal words, opting instead to address their deeper needs. He understood that because words flow from a person's heart (Matt. 12:33–37), he couldn't take conversations merely at face value, but had to take a person's heart into account when he responded.

Our Hearts Don't Always Want What Jesus Offers

The sixth chapter of John records a protracted, heartbreaking discussion between Jesus and a large crowd. Jesus had been caring for them by teaching them, feeding them, and healing those who were sick, and in return they couldn't get enough of him. He crossed the Sea of Galilee that night, and they followed him around it the next day.

But they did so for the wrong reason, and Jesus knew it. So essentially he told them, "You're not interested in me. You're interested in what you think I'll give you. You want a free lunch" (see John 6:26). They didn't like hearing that, so they began to argue, "No, we really want you," but as you read the passage, they undermined their claim by repeatedly trying to wheedle a meal out of him (John 6:30–31, 34).

It's a frightening passage: here's Jesus, the real food they need, come down from heaven sent by the Father, standing right in front of them, and they don't want him. They want something else because they already had an idea of what made a good life and he wasn't part of their definition.

More than that, he was irritating. He insisted on taking up their time with a philosophical-theological discussion while they were hungry. And so they found ways to discount the truth of what he was saying—"It's just Jesus, the carpenter's son" (see John 6:42).

They had convinced themselves that what they wanted was right and best, and so they conjured up reasons for why they should reject what he offered. Those reasons let them continue believing, "If only I had a little lunch, then my life would be good. And Jesus could easily give me that, but he won't. He's distracting me with all this nonsense about how he would satisfy my real hunger when I already know what would satisfy me." Their internal commitment to their stomachs drove their end of the conversation.

And that scares me because I know I'm just like them. When faced with Jesus, the true source of life, I find myself at times wanting something else, anything else, other than Jesus. I know I'm not alone. Don't you find moments when you are convinced that if only you had a little more in your bank account, a house full of stuff, a longer vacation, more friends, better friends, a better job, a spouse who smiled at you when you came home, or your kids' respect, then life would finally be satisfying?

That's evil in its most fundamental form. It's a restless poison deep inside that never stops crying out, turning away from what God offers. Evil not only hates who God is, it hates his provision. It wants more than God offers, but it especially wants different than God offers. You need Jesus to live, but you don't always want Jesus. That's evil.

And that's what Jesus was trying to help the crowd see—that their physical preoccupation with another meal was overshadowing the real need of their spiritual hunger. If we don't engage our kids at the level of their heart longings, then we'll find ourselves in endless circular conversations that never invite them to know the goodness of the gospel or how it addresses their true needs.

Help Your Children See That They Can't Change Their Own Hearts

One afternoon our son Danny pressed Sally to go to the pet store over and over. He was upset because they hadn't gone the previous night despite being told they would, and he was determined that history was not going to repeat itself. He was getting ramped up—double- and triple-checking when they would go, making sure his mom had it on her agenda, letting her know how unhappy he was that they hadn't gone yesterday, and adding more and more energy with each interaction.

Sal was doing her best to reassure him, but she was getting frustrated because nothing she said helped him calm down. After overhearing their conversation go back and forth for a while, I called Dan into my office, and we talked about how there was nothing inherently wrong with wanting to go to the store, that it was a good thing even—when the desire was the right size.

And so borrowing a page from James 4:1–3, I talked about how good things can become bad when they become too important to us and how we always end up ruining our relationships when that happens because people are no longer images of God to be valued and cared for. Instead, they either become helps or hindrances to our goal.

I said, "When going to the store gets too big, then Mom is great because she takes you and you are thrilled to have this wonderful mom. Or, if she won't, then she's mean and standing in your way and you need to move her out of your way with your words. Either way, you're no longer relating to her; you're just trying to use her."

He nodded thoughtfully, so I asked, "So . . . what do you want to do about this?"

"Put it out of my mind and stop thinking about it?"

I smiled at him, but shook my head. "No," I said, "you can't—that's the problem when good things get too big; they're out of your control, and you can't make them smaller. But Jesus can help. Tell him you're sorry. Ask his forgiveness for letting a good thing get too big. Then ask him not to take away your desire, but to shrink it back down to the right size so that it doesn't get in the way between you and Mom anymore."

The gospel is the solution to every problem of living. Daily, you and your kids will fixate on wanting something more than you want Jesus, but there's hope because Jesus died to free you both from that thing inside of you that rejects him. More than that, he rose from the dead and filled you with his Spirit so that you can now long for him more than you long for anything else.

He is what you really need in very practical ways today, but you'll only see your need—and your kids will only see their need—when your conversations go below the surface and engage their hearts.

28

Lead with Your Worst Foot Forward

You need to challenge your kids at the level of their hearts when they engage in false worship so that they can see their true need of Christ. But that challenge will expose them, and if you're not careful, will leave them feeling insecure and unprotected.

How can you invite them to a place of vulnerability that they'd be willing to embrace? You go there first. You make yourself more vulnerable than you're inviting them to be. You make clear to them that you are in just as much need as they are and that consequently, if there's hope for you, then surely there's hope for them. That's what Paul does in his letter to the Christians in Rome.

Paul hadn't personally met his Roman brothers and sisters, but that didn't stop him from being brutally honest about his need of Christ. Here's a brief glimpse of himself from the letter he wrote them:

> For we know that the law is spiritual, but I am of the flesh, sold under sin. For I do not understand my own actions. For I do not do what I want, but I do the very thing I hate. Now if

I do what I do not want, I agree with the law, that it is good. So now it is no longer I who do it, but sin that dwells within me. For I know that nothing good dwells in me, that is, in my flesh. For I have the desire to do what is right, but not the ability to carry it out. For I do not do the good I want, but the evil I do not want is what I keep on doing. Now if I do what I do not want, it is no longer I who do it, but sin that dwells within me. (Rom. 7:14–20)

Listen carefully. The master theologian who explored the mystery of Christ and wrote much of our New Testament Scriptures just said, "I do not understand my own actions—what I'm doing doesn't make a bit of sense to me. It's crazy to do the things I hate to do. I don't get it" (see 7:15).

You can hear Paul's confusion and frustration in the way he writes in circles: "For I do not do what I want, but I do the very thing I hate. Now if I do what I do not want, I agree with the law, that it is good" (Rom. 7:15–16).

It's as if he's saying, "I like what I see in the law. I agree with it. I know that if I loved my neighbor as myself, then this would be a good world to live in, and I want that good world. I want a world where you trust me and I trust you. I want a world where I want the best for you and don't want to use you. I want a world where I am honest with you and where you are honest with me because we both know that we will not hurt each other with what we know about each other. I want kids to experience that world and grow up in that world and become that world . . . and yet I ruin that world."

There is a deep soul-struggle within Paul that is not past but present. Notice the verb tense. Paul is writing about right now, in the present. This is not a historical, abstract wrestling that he is describing. It is a present, restless, ongoing, personal struggle.

You can hear him saying, "Instead of doing good, I do what I hate. I do the things that ruin relationship. I spend more time thinking about what I want to say than about what you are trying to talk about. I promote myself endlessly. I run over top of you.

I ignore you. I obsess over things you've done to me, and I hold them tightly in my mind, refusing to let them go. I think long and hard about how to get back at you and make you pay. And none of it is ever satisfying and it only drives us away from each other. I hate it *and* I do it" (see v. 19).

It all starts to sound hopeless until you realize that Paul's true self—the "me" of verses 17 and 20 that really counts—is no longer wrapped up in doing evil. There's been an internal change. It's as if Paul is saying, "I can still do bad things, but I don't love doing them. Instead, I want to do something different. I desire something so much better. My fundamental identity is not in being ugly to you but in being good to you, and that's where the confusion enters in. There's this other thing—sin—that lives inside of the 'me' that really counts as me."

He's explicit enough with his struggle, that we all recognize the same wrestling in ourselves and can identify with him. But then he points us beyond the struggle to a deeper reality: we've been given a new nature by the God who rescued us. As you keep reading Paul's letter, you learn that this God will never give up on you or allow anything to get in between him and the new "me" he has made you (Rom. 8:31–38).

That's the payoff. Paul's been sharing some ugly stuff, but despite how bad things really are, none of it is bad enough to keep Christ away from him—which means there isn't anything bad enough in you to keep Christ away from you either.

And that goes a bit counter to the way some of us think. I can imagine someone thousands of years ago saying, "You know Paul, you've got some issues here. There're some things you need to take care of before you're going to be of any value to anyone else. So maybe you should get some help. You know, see a counselor or something. Once you're straightened out, then you'll be ready to minister to other people."

Paul understands a deeper truth: he will never be beyond his need of Jesus, but that reality doesn't disqualify him from ministry.

Rather, it can make ministry possible as he builds a relationship with people he's never met on the basis of his and their shared need of Christ. His struggles don't isolate him from others. They are the bridge that connects him to fellow strugglers who need the same gospel hope that he himself has.

Speaking about your own experiences of needing Christ is an important part of calling your children to experience grace on their own. That means if you're not willing to use your stories of failure to help them as much as Paul uses his to help you, you need to ask yourself why.

Convince Your Children That You Need Jesus Just as Much as They Do

I'd been watching my son, Tim, over several days increasingly lose control of his life: spending endless time watching videos on his phone, scattering his belongings all over the house, inhaling any and all baked goods in huge quantities—in short, living a life without limits.

I knew I needed to bring this to his attention, but I also knew it could easily feel demoralizing, especially if I came across as having my act together. So I chose to tell him about a recent night where I had lost all self-control.

Sunday nights can be a real struggle for me with the television. As a pastor, Sunday is the end of my week, and instead of being a day that eases into my day off, it's the point toward which my whole week has been building. It's a very public day shared with several hundred people that often climaxes with preaching two services. At the end of it, all I want is some kind of numb, and the TV promises to deliver just that.

It's so easy to mindlessly surf the channels, moving from one station to the next to the next to the next—not because I care about any of the things I'm watching, but because when I'm watching, I don't have to think, I don't have to feel, and I don't have to process the day. It's essentially an electronic drug. And just like other numbing drugs, you can never get enough.

So I told Tim about the night when I had been bouncing back and forth between *The World Series* and *Sunday Night Football* till they both ended, at which point I started in on reruns of *Elementary* and *Person of Interest.* And I told him about how I knew I needed to stop and just go to bed, but I kept watching anyway while the clock hands spun around from 11:00 to 11:30 to 12:00 until I was finally able to turn it off at 12:30. It sounds ridiculous, but I needed the power of God to manage even that. That's the level of my need.

It was helpful for Tim to hear he's not alone in his struggles, and that I get how impossible it feels to say no to yourself—and that Jesus doesn't abandon us even then. We can still run to him for help and change because he still loves us.

We had a good conversation without any hint of defensiveness. It was similar to other times when I've told on myself for gossiping, bullying, being violent, stealing, eating too much, drinking too much, seeing things I shouldn't, lying, and manipulating.

Similar to the apostle Paul's experience, I've seen those confessions build bridges simply by acknowledging what is obvious to everyone: that I don't have my act together, but I know someone who loves me anyway and is working overtime to change me.

Being vulnerable has also had the unexpected effect of getting help for me. The very next Sunday after our conversation, Tim poked his head into the den on his way to bed and said, "Make sure you get to bed before 12:30 tonight, okay?"

And I did. But only because I had someone boldly step into my world to speak honestly to me—someone who understands my weaknesses and has learned to step into places with his words to help others who struggle the same way he does. Without him, I'm pretty sure I wouldn't have made it that night.

You need what you're offering to your kids. And they need to know that you're aware of your own needs and even more aware of your Savior, who meets each one.

29

Build Bridges with Your Failures

Maybe you're a little nervous about telling your kids some of your past struggles. You might be thinking like one mother who told me, "I'm afraid if I share too much about my past, then my kid will either think that what he's doing is okay because I did it and turned out okay, or he'll lose respect for me for what I've done."

The apostle Paul seems to think the risk is worth it. Not only does he describe his struggles in Romans, but elsewhere he willingly confesses what he's done to qualify as the "foremost" of sinners (1 Tim. 1:15). When I read those passages, I never feel like I get a free pass to sin, and my esteem for Paul only goes up each time he risks his reputation just to help me see Jesus a little better.

That's been my experience with my children as well. If anything, they seem to respect me more and are more open to sharing their lives as I share mine. That said, there are several things you learn in Scripture that should guide how you talk with your children about your past.

First, you need to be detailed enough that your kids believe you really understand what it's like to be in their shoes, but not so detailed that you're inviting them to sin vicariously through your retelling.

When God tells you the story of David seducing Bathsheba in 2 Samuel 11, you know exactly what happened as he looked at her from across the rooftops, but never once are you given details that border on the pornographic. The story doesn't incite your imagination or entice you to stand alongside David and indulge yourself in sexualized fantasies as he did.

Rather, you know what happened and you're repulsed. The way the story is told, nothing David does is the least bit attractive. From his dereliction of duty to his voyeurism to his multiple faithless betrayals, it's all ugly and you feel it.

As you share your stories of failure with your kids, be careful that you don't unintentionally make evil look good or enjoyable or worthwhile or amusing or rewarding. Guard your heart especially from the temptation to make yourself look clever or powerful or bold or witty or desirable.

Stories of gossip and slander should not end with you having the last word. Stories of bullying must not end with the other person getting what they deserved. Stories of stealing can't end with you profiting. Stories of sexual or business conquests can't end with you being successful.

Stories of sin need to show the brokenness that results from refusing to live God's way in God's world. Point out the horizontal effects of depravity, how you brought harm to others and also to yourself. Don't forget to talk about the internal consequences that are harder to see, like feelings of guilt, regret, sadness, embarrassment, shame, or even worse, a seared and hardened conscience.

In other words, talk about what you did in a way that lays bare the true, ugly nature of evil for what it is (Eph. 5:11). When you do that, your children will not want to run to sin to try it out for themselves. Rather, they will long for redemption, for someone who will come and redeem what you have ruined.

That's when, secondly, you tell them of the Redeemer. Tell your story in such a way that Jesus is the hero and not you; otherwise, you'll teach your kids that they're supposed to be the future heroes of their own stories. That means you don't tell them stories to "scare them straight" based on the things that happened to you. Nor do you spin modern parables and cautionary tales that end with a moralistic lesson: "Don't be like me when I was your age." The only reason you're willing to delve into your past is to show how you've needed a God who rescues sinners from the false worship to which they've enslaved themselves. That's the real story of Scripture. It's not about human paragons of virtue who triumph or case studies of villains that meet bad ends. It's about a righteous, redeeming God who breaks into his people's lives, against all odds, in order to rescue them and restore what they've broken. Telling your story any other way puts it outside the narrative arc of what Jesus is doing throughout human history.

You Need to Reexperience the Gospel When Your Kids See You Fail

Years ago, a friend reminded me of the crucial role our words play in helping people see this Jesus who invades our worlds. That conversation made me wonder how well my wife and I were doing in communicating him to our children. So, when in doubt, ask. As we were all having lunch together one Sunday, talking about how important our words are, I asked, "Where do you guys think Mommy and I are good at helping you see Jesus when we talk to you?"

The kids talked about ways they experienced us being kind, compassionate, and loving with them. Then Cass added, "You also help us see him more clearly when you forgive us . . . well, Mommy does anyway." Then looking at me she said, "You're not as good at that."

I nodded. "Yeah, you're right. She is much better at that than I am. And I'm really glad you said that because you're moving us to the second question I wanted to ask: where do the three of you see us still needing to grow in showing Christ to you?"

They had lots of things to say that had the potential to help Sally and me become better parents. It was a good conversation, and yet there was also a hidden danger that had the potential to undermine our parenting. It would have been so easy for us to ignore the gospel and turn their comments into moralistic admonitions like, "Dad, work harder at forgiving."

Now, do I need to grow in my ability to forgive? Absolutely. But can I do that apart from my Redeemer? Not at all. The path away from moralism lies first in connecting with Christ. The reason I'm so bad at forgiving is that I don't fully appreciate or experience being forgiven. If I did, it would flow more naturally from Christ to me to my children.

That doesn't give me license to be bitter and standoffish when I'm upset with my kids. But when I refuse to forgive them, my coldness toward them needs to make me aware of how much I need the God whose death and resurrection erases my sin.

What's happening when I'm icy toward my kids? I'm trying to make them pay for what they've done by freezing them out relationally. In that moment, it's not they who most need my forgiveness. It's I who most needs God's. I'm no longer trying to enter their worlds and treat them as I've been treated. Instead, I'm withholding from them the very thing that I've been so glad to receive.

That means I need to experience God's forgiveness again for my hard heart and be amazed one more time at his endless grace in my life and his commitment to me. I need to experience one more time the reality that nothing can separate me from him (Rom. 8:31–38)—not even my present unkindness to my family. And interacting with him, being forgiven, changes me. I become quicker to forgive as I realize how much I've been forgiven. And I become more willing to hear that I still have a long way to go.

It is nothing less than a miracle of his grace that my family could have that conversation around the lunch table that afternoon. For far too long I thought constructive criticism was kind of an oxymoron: people could be either constructive or critical, but not both. Since I built my value and personal identity on how well I was doing in life, I couldn't stand hearing about times when I wasn't doing well. That's a recipe for disaster as a parent.

How do you go from being that kind of a closed, defensive guy to someone who is willing to hear his kids say, "Yeah, you're not such a great dad at times"? It's knowing that nothing can separate you from the love of God. What changed me—what keeps changing me—is the Word of God, spoken from the Father to me, his child.

His words help me know his heart: that I am absolutely safe with him. That my reputation is secure because he has my back. That I am far more deeply loved than I have yet dared to imagine. That he is working in me now and will not quit until I am pure and perfect, just like Christ. That he has taken away every wrong thing that I've ever done to him, along with the penalty of doing wrong. That at this very moment he is not angry with me. That he likes me and wants to be friends with me.

And as the reality of what he says filters down into my soul, I don't mind telling you about where I've been and what I've done, not so that you'll be impressed with me, but so that you'll be impressed with him. Your kids need to hear the same from you, especially in those moments when you need to speak honestly to them about their failings.

30

Expect Your Kids to Make Mistakes

Every day as a parent requires you to speak up because one of your kids has messed up. You may not feel prepared, but you have to say something when your child:

- has run all the water out of the hot water tank . . . again, or worse,
- has been teaching his little brother special words that you don't use and you don't think ought to be used, or even worse,
- has been misusing computer search engines to look for things that no one should see.

In other words, you will need to say something every day because every day your kids will create a problem for themselves or for someone else.

But some days you just don't want to wade in one more time and say anything. Sometimes you're tired of saying the same things over and over and being ignored. Sometimes you're confused and have no idea what to say. And then there are times when you know that what you want to say won't be good to say. What do you do then?

That's when you need to remind yourself that you and your kids are normal, but your God is exceptional. Hebrews 5:1–3 meets you in that place:

> For every high priest chosen from among men is appointed to act on behalf of men in relation to God, to offer gifts and sacrifices for sins. He can deal gently with the ignorant and wayward, since he himself is beset with weakness. Because of this he is obligated to offer sacrifice for his own sins just as he does for those of the people.

Notice that the Old Testament priests were just like the people they served—subject to weakness. The Greek word translated "weakness" packs a really strong punch. It means something like: our basic human condition that makes us vulnerable to give in when tempted by sin or when we are suffering.

It's that experience of being subject to weakness that moves a priest to deal gently with people. Priests know how hard it is to live a holy life. They walk in human shoes, and they get how hard it is to do it well.

They also know that they need a sacrifice for themselves (Heb. 5:3). They need what they offer to others, and that keeps them from looking down on anyone else in need. Their firsthand experience with weakness moves them to treat others gently.

Oddly enough, part of what was true of mere human priests is also true of our divine-human priest. That word "weakness" showed up a few verses earlier in Hebrews 4:15, where we learn something about Jesus: "For we do not have a high priest who is unable to sympathize with our weaknesses [same word as in 5:2], but one who in every respect has been tempted as we are, yet without sin."

Jesus empathizes with you because he knows exactly how hard it is to for you to live with your human weaknesses. That's why he spent more than three decades on this planet. Did you ever wonder why he didn't just show up for the crucifixion? If all he needed to do was simply die for our sin, why did he bother being born and go through all the things that he did for as long as he did?

It's because he needed this insider knowledge, the experience of the human condition, so that he could be the right kind of High Priest for you after he rose from the dead.

If he didn't know how hard it was to be you, you might be tempted to think, "Okay, since God has no firsthand experience with being human, he can't possibly know how hard it is to live on this planet and do what's right. If he doesn't know what weakness is like, I probably shouldn't expect a whole lot from him. At some point he'll get fed up and decide I'm just not worth the trouble."

You can never think that because Jesus does know how hard it is for you. He doesn't look down on you when you struggle. Instead, he feels what you feel—that's what empathy means—because he's lived it already. He may not have had your exact experiences, but over the thirty-plus years he lived here, he had enough of his own experiences that he has felt every temptation that you've ever had.

- He knows the frustration of a conversation that doesn't start well, doesn't go well, and doesn't end well.
- He knows the uncertainty of wondering whether or not the other person will actually hear what you're saying.
- He knows the discouragement of feeling like you're having the same conversation you've had a dozen times before because the other person *still* doesn't get it.
- He knows the temptation to just nod and agree so that you can get the whole thing over with.
- He understands how you are tempted to hammer home your points, only say half of what you think you need to say, or simply quit, give up, and walk away.

He was tempted in every way you are because of what he experienced. And the best part? His experience didn't harden him.

He'll never say to you, "Look, I did it. It was hard, yeah, but I made it, so just gut it out." Instead, he sympathizes with you. Because he knows what you feel from the inside, you can be sure he'll help you when you ask (Heb. 4:16). He deals with you gently, just like any human priest should (Heb. 5:2).

Jesus Purchased You to Deal Gently with Others Like He Does with You

And then this same Jesus turns around and makes you into the same kind of priest that he is. That's part of what he is praised for by heavenly creatures in the throne room of God. Listen to what they say to him in Revelation 5:9–10:

> Worthy are you to take the scroll
>   and to open its seals,
> for you were slain, and by your blood you ransomed people
>   for God
>   from every tribe and language and people and nation,
> and you have made them a kingdom and priests to our God,
>   and they shall reign on the earth.

Jesus purchased you with his blood to make you a priest who now serves our God. That's you. You're now a priest who serves others in the same way Jesus serves you. You engage people, especially your children, the way Jesus engages you.

And so Hebrews 5:2 becomes a model for your conversations: dealing gently with people who are ignorant and wayward, or as the NIV puts it, "ignorant and going astray." Since the passage describes the kind of high priest that anticipated who Jesus would be, and since this is the kind of High Priest that Jesus is, then this is the kind of priest that Jesus makes you.

That means you learn not to be surprised when people are ignorant and going astray. Instead, you expect it. You realize that it's part of the human condition. People—including Christians; including your children—are ignorant and going astray.

Sometimes they have no idea that what they're doing is a bad thing—they're clueless, ignorant. And sometimes they do have an idea, but they do it anyway—they're willful, going astray.

Ignorant and going astray is one way of summing up the problem of the human race. It's what gets in the way of knowing God because it clashes with his holiness. It gets in the way of relating to each other because one person's ignorant waywardness sets them on a collision course with everyone else's ignorant waywardness. And that's true of every single person you're going to talk to today. Each one has a tendency to be ignorant and going astray.

Your friends are ignorant and going astray. Your spouse is ignorant and going astray. Your neighbors are ignorant and going astray. Your coworkers are ignorant and going astray. You are ignorant and going astray. And your child is ignorant and going astray.

That's true, and it's not what any of us wants to hear. We want relationships with people who are not ignorant or going astray. We want relationships where the other person does the right thing most of the time and we don't have to say anything to him.

Someone in my family was frustrated one day and blurted out, "Why is he so annoying?" Now, there are three men in my home and one male cat, and "he" could have been any one of the four of us that was annoying.

That's the way we are. That's the way we come, and that's frustrating to the people who have to live with us. But it's even more frustrating if you don't expect us to be annoying.

That's what the annoyed person was saying. In his mind, the annoying person is not supposed to be annoying. He's supposed to be relatively easy to get along with. He's not supposed to cause frustration. And because the person who is annoyed is not expecting others to be hard to get along with, he blurts out, "Why is he so annoying?"

In that moment, the frustrated person is not speaking like a priest because he is not expecting the rest of us to be ignorant and going astray.

What do you and I need in the moment that we're annoying? We need one of those priests that Jesus purchased. We don't need someone who will offer sacrifices for us—Jesus has already done that, once for all time—but someone who will enter into our annoying moments with words that are helpful, not hurtful. We need someone to enter into our weakness and our sin, and point us in a better direction. That's what Christ purchased you for—for when the people around you are annoying.

But you won't be that priest if you expect people not to be ignorant and going astray. I know of an engineer who was incredibly patient whenever the appliances broke in the house. He took them apart, located the problem, and put them back together. He was very patient with things, but not very patient with the people who lived in the house. One of those people, trying to make sense of his reality said to me, "It's because he doesn't expect machines to work right, but he does expect people to work right."

You will never be a priest if you expect people to work right. I'm not saying that it's okay for someone to be ignorant and going astray. It's not okay—it's unholy. But it's not a surprise—you should expect it.

That means that as a blood-bought priest, you have to communicate that you still want to be involved with annoying people even when they don't work right. Part of parenting involves going out of your way to let your kids know that you can handle their failings well. If you let them know you'll handle them badly, that doesn't mean they'll stop having problems. It just means that you won't get to know about the problems they have.

When Timmy was a preschooler, he told us about a playdate he'd had at a friend's house in the winter and how they were breaking up ice chunks together. He said, "There was dirt on the ice, and I ate some of it," but then quickly added, "But the piece

I ate didn't have any dirt on it!" Oh, for the days when living on the edge means you're out in the backyard sneaking dirty ice.

The same day, Cass came home from first grade and had to tell us that she got busted at school for having a pocketknife in her desk . . . that she had stolen out of my briefcase. As this was just a couple of years after 9/11, that lapse of judgment really didn't go over well with the school.

Two worlds, colliding at my dinner table: Timmy eating ice without permission; Cassie packing weapons without permission. Worlds that I listened to with the same level of calmness.

Now, calm does not mean apathetic. We discussed Cass's situation thoroughly. But I wanted to do so in a way that said to my family, "I want to hear your problems, not drive you away." See, if I react badly to the times when people are ignorant and going astray, they'll still be ignorant and going astray; I just won't get to hear about it.

Cassie told me several weeks later that she was surprised that I hadn't yelled at her for the knife incident. To which I said, "Well, how would that have helped if I had?" My goal is to react in such a way that I get to help pick up the pieces that my family makes. You can only do that if you're expecting them to make pieces— if you're expecting them to be ignorant and going astray.

Priests Look for Gospel Opportunities— Both for Others and for Themselves

You can't make someone want Jesus. But moments of ignorance and waywardness are good moments because it's clear that the other person cannot make his life work without him. Those are the moments for which you were made a priest because in that moment, your child needs someone to gently call him back to Christ.

Don't wish those moments away. Don't sigh or frown or look surprised when they come up. Don't long for low-maintenance kids who never need you to step in and say anything. Stop wishing you were raising Pharisees—kids who look good on the outside but are in deep trouble inside.

Jesus did not purchase you with his blood so that you could waste your time wishing you had an easy life—a life of being utterly useless to the people around you. He purchased you with his blood so that you could be a priest who deals gently with people who are ignorant and going astray.

That means when you don't want to start a conversation that steps into the messes people make and you don't want to direct them back to the God they need, then you need the same thing you're offering them. You need his sacrifice again, because in that moment you are ignorant and going astray because you're not living the life he purchased for you.

The good news is that he still deals gently with you. He's not going to let you get away with checking out of life, because he has much better plans for you. Trust him to deal gently with you so that you can deal gently with others.

Ask him for help when you don't want to have one more conversation. Ask him to forgive you for not wanting to speak. Ask him to give you love for your child who is in need, and ask him to give you words that will let your children experience what it's like to be treated in a God-like, gentle manner.

31

Extended Story: Catching a Line Drive . . . or Not

My middle son Timmy made a lot of pieces one night that he needed help picking up.

He was playing center field in a baseball tournament when a line drive threatened to rocket over his head. I thought, "Uh oh, that's trouble," and fully expected to see him go sprinting after it. Instead, I watched in amazement as he coiled himself into the ground and launched himself, arm outstretched, into the air, snagged the ball, then fell back down.

The parents went wild. The umpire signaled "out." The inning was over, and the boys ran off the field.

But the other team challenged the call. Tim had shifted his glove hand oddly as he gathered himself up from the ground, and the other team was arguing that he dropped the ball.

Instead of backing his initial call, the ump dumped his responsibility on a ten-year-old. Set up behind the plate, he was a long way from deep center and hadn't seen the whole play clearly. So he walked over to Timmy and asked him if he had caught it.

Surrounded by three coaches and ten fellow teammates in a close game, Tim said, "Yes." But I wasn't sure. I was a lot closer to the outfield, and it really did look like he scrambled to stuff something back into his glove.

After the game ended, I walked with him back to the van, praising him for all his good plays, especially that play—which really was amazing even if he had dropped it. Bending down, I got eye level with him and said, "Tell me something. Did you really catch that ball, or did it roll out?"

"No, I really caught it."

"Okay," I said not really believing him, "but listen to me. I just want you to know that if you ever do something wrong . . . like lie about catching a ball when you didn't, you can tell me. Okay?"

"Okay," he replied.

I figured that was the end of it. When we got home, he and his sister hung out and followed me all around as I watered the garden then wandered through the house to my office and logged onto the computer. Finally Cass went off to get something to eat, and that's when Tim spoke up, "Dad? Remember you said I could tell you anything?"

"Yeah," I said.

With tears in his eyes he told me how his glove slipped off his hand after he caught the ball before he landed on the ground— it was a really hard hit! He talked about how pandemonium broke out around him. How everyone on his team was telling him what a really great catch it was. The other team was shouting that it wasn't. The ump was asking him questions. And his coach told him he didn't have to answer.

And all he wanted in that moment was for people to think that he had made a great catch. So under all that pressure—both internal and external—he told them what they wanted to hear, even though he didn't believe it. And immediately he hated doing it. He felt the heavy weight that comes from lying. He felt like his team didn't deserve to win, and he was secretly hoping they wouldn't.

And I just listened, more proud of him than when he laid out for the ball. He wasn't owning up to something wrong because he got caught. Quite the opposite. He had gotten away with it. But he wasn't okay with it. Far from being hardened, his conscience was working the way God designed it. And so here he was, courageously letting me see the real Tim. That took at least as much courage as it would have to have owned the truth in front of his team.

But it also took an invitation that he thought was worth the risk of admitting he had lied. "If you hadn't told me I could come to you, I wouldn't have," he said, "but I thought about what you said all the way home, and I couldn't wait to talk to you." He thanked me for that invitation and shared his relief that I wasn't angry with him.

How could I be? I told him of a recent event where I had embellished the truth so that people would laugh at the story I was telling. I told him how I had realized that their laughter was more important to me in that moment than God's enjoyment of how I told the story. I talked about how I had gotten away with it and how I had hated myself afterward, about how Tim and I are not all that different.

So we prayed together, asking Jesus to forgive him, but also celebrating God's work in him to open up the dark corners of his life that he could have kept secret.

To know and experience the grace of God means that your children, your spouse, your friends, your coworkers, and everyone you know will get in trouble—otherwise, how would they know the depths of the riches of his kindness (Rom. 11:32)? You are the first experience of what his kindness and grace look like and feel like.

Please don't live for your kids to be perfect. Live instead for them to experience perfect love through their imperfections. As you give them a taste of what that kind of love is like, it will signal to them what they can expect from their God. Rather than recoiling in shock when they mess up, use words that embrace the moment by embracing them.

32

Why You Really Do Want
a Forgiving Lifestyle

The hard reality of life on this planet is that your children will sin against you and you will sin against your children. That means if you're to have any hope of building an ongoing relationship with them, then forgiveness is a daily necessity.

Sadly, however, forgiveness is a hard commodity to come by. Forgiveness is costly. You have to let go of your demand to make someone pay for how difficult he's made your life. The alternatives—placate, ignore, gloss over, explode, remain bitter, demand penance—are much more common because they let you pass along the cost to the person who did the wrong. You end up trying to make your kids pay even though both you and they know that they can't fully.

Given our firsthand experience of how hard it is to forgive, you'd think that we'd give God credit that it's even harder for him. We don't. We subtly believe that because he's God, it should be easier for him, which leads us to take his forgiveness for granted. We treat him as if he's less of a person than we are and, therefore, less personally invested in his world than we are in ours.

I've been rebuilding my house for over a decade now. No, it's not that big; it was in that bad a condition before we moved in. At this point it's still not finished, but I'm proud of what we've done. Proud and more than a little protective. I've been known to get incensed when my young people would pick at the paint, write on the walls, scratch up the floor, bang the doors, or run through the flower beds. Didn't they realize what they were doing? Didn't they realize how long it had taken me to make the place nicer?

It was especially hard to take when they did the same destructive thing the second, third, and even more times. I'd get loud, complain, withdraw, or mope around in self-pity refusing to talk to people.

That's only one small quarter acre that I've worked on for a few years. What would it be like to pour yourself into the universe over countless eons creating a visible representation of your own glory, only to have your children willfully trash it? Take any example you want where you've labored long and hard to create something you liked. Now imagine someone ruining it, and think about how easy it would be for you to release him from what he did. Think about how hard it would be to want to have anything to do with him.

When we treat our own sins lightly or glibly ask God to forgive us, we assume that forgiveness is much easier for him than for us. A little thought shows it's actually much harder. So, why would he choose to burden himself with the cost of forgiving us? Psalm 32:1–2 holds a clue:

> Blessed is the one whose transgression is forgiven,
>   whose sin is covered.
> Blessed is the man against whom the Lord counts no
>   iniquity,
>   and in whose spirit there is no deceit.

Why forgive someone? Because then that person is blessed. Think about what it would mean if the Lord counted your sin against you. It would mean that he holds you responsible for what you've done, for the effect that it's had on him, on you, and on others, and that he holds you responsible for paying for all those effects. You'd be responsible for undoing all the damage you've caused so that no trace of it remains. In other words, if he counts your sins against you, you're holding a debt you've generated that's impossible to pay off.

Additionally, sin is the expression of an inner desire to be free of God, his ways, his traits, his characteristics, and his attributes as they're expressed in a physical universe. In short, your sin and mine expresses our rejection of him, for which hell is the logical endpoint as it is the complete opposite of him; it's the complete absence of his goodness and grace. Hell is the appropriate reward for wanting nothing to do with God.

Do you see now why you are blessed when God doesn't count your sin against you? You've called down hell on your own head, and God has stepped in so that you don't get what you've asked for. You get him instead. Forgiveness from him indicates that his desire for relationship with you is greater than his fury at what you've done. He'd rather pay the cost that you've incurred than have you be cut off from him. When you extend forgiveness to your children, not counting their sins against them, you communicate the same message.

But what if you don't want to forgive? What if you don't feel like it? What if you think you've done more than your fair share and that you are now past Jesus's famous seventy-times-seven?

Start by letting yourself be scared. Recognize the danger you're putting yourself in, because at this moment you are deciding that you have a better way of living with people than the one God chooses with you.

Worse, realize that you've tasted the sweetness of being forgiven. You know what it's like not to be burdened with debts you can never pay, to know that nothing stands between you and God. You've enjoyed the lightness of not carrying your guilt, and yet, you won't allow someone else to taste that experience from you.

In the moment of your unforgiveness, you're returning evil to another for the good you have received. In short, you're sinning. Again. You're ringing up another debt that you cannot pay. And in the moment that you refuse to forgive, you now need to be forgiven. Again.

In other words, you stand in as much need as your child. Maybe more. Your child has sinned against an image of God. You've decided to go for the Original himself. They may be your children, but he is your parent.

Despite all this, he still doesn't treat you as your sins deserve. Why? Because in not making you pay, he's telling you how serious he is about wanting a friendship with you. So go. Get blessed by God, asking him one more time not to count your sin against you. Then go and bless others—your children—in return.

Afterword

You're a Megaphone

You are a megaphone. You are made in God's image, and therefore, you speak with greater weight—for glory or shame—than you often realize because you speak as his visible representative on earth. You can't help it. Even if you were to pull away and not speak for fear of saying the wrong thing, your silence would be deafening, and therefore, devastating to those around you.

Words are powerful. Early in humanity's history, the serpent used his voice in the garden of Eden to sow doubt and mistrust among us that grew into broken relationships, first with God and then with everyone else. It's frightening how quickly Adam turned on Eve and Eve on the serpent whom she had just befriended after they had both turned on God. Sin shreds relationships.

Grace, however, restores them, using a different set of words. His words invite, call out, woo, and pursue, giving a sense of what a grace-based relationship could be like. It's an invitation that we'd be foolish to refuse for ourselves and inexcusable not to offer to those around us.

I walked into the house after church one Sunday afternoon and was immediately aware that something was very wrong. The house just felt heavy. Sally and Danny were sitting side by side on the living room couch, but no one was talking. Danny got up slowly, shuffled over to me, never once picked his head up, and stood silently in front of me.

"Hey, buddy," I said, reaching out to hug him to me. "What's wrong?"

His voice broke as he mumbled, "I broke your mug."

Oh. Now it made sense. I was given a fancy tea mug by a class I taught in Korea a number of years back. It was intricately decorated and distinctly Asian—a special gift that the students all chipped in for to show their appreciation to the visiting professor.

This mug had become a staple of daily living in our household. I grew up drinking tea every morning. Then I married a Brit, so we have tea at least twice a day, whether we need it or not, and always from our favorite mugs. Now, apparently, this one was no longer going to be part of our daily ritual, and Danny was deeply upset.

I stroked his hair to soothe him and waited until words had a chance to sink in. It's taken me far too long to realize that the gospel has a sense of rhythm and timing. Until people are feeling relatively at ease in your presence, words don't make a bit of sense to them. When he was calmer, I said, "You're right. My mug is special to me, but you are far more special."

He clung to me more tightly, then we went to look at the damage. While it would never be functional again, I told him the mug could be glued together and decorate one of our bookshelves. We then washed up with the rest of the family and sat down for lunch. Trying to get past the cloud that was still hanging over us, I primed the conversation with our standard Sunday morning question: "So, how did we see Jesus this morning?"

And Danny immediately responded, "You."

I wasn't sure what to do with that—adopt some sense of false humility? Pretend I don't like being equated with Jesus? Assume I know exactly what he means? Disregard what's moving his heart because I'm uncomfortable?

None of those options build honest relationship—the kind that Jesus builds with me—so I thought maybe it'd be best to let him share more of himself. Taking a page from God's relational handbook, I tried a question, "How do you mean?"

"Well," he said, "I broke your mug, and you didn't get mad at me. That's like Jesus."

"That's cool." I said, "You know though, he's lots better. You broke my mug by accident and I didn't get angry. We break his world on purpose and he doesn't mistreat us." We all paused then as the reality of God's amazing kindness sank in a little bit more deeply than it had before.

I would gladly sacrifice my mug, or any of my possessions, for the chance of having conversations like that one. Actually, I don't have to. You don't either. Every single interaction we have communicates what most grips our heart, what we value most highly, what controls us, and what shapes how we will treat others. Therefore, all day, every day, we are constantly given normal, ordinary opportunities to say three very important things:

- "This is the kind of person I am."
- "This is the kind of relationship you can expect to have with me in the future."
- "This is a little taste of the God I know."

Each of those statements comes with an implicit invitation:

- "Do you think I am someone worth knowing?"
- "Do you want to keep building this friendship with me?"
- "Would you like to know more of this God that I'm getting to know?"

The stakes are too high to ignore the importance of what we're communicating. Sadly, like you, I've said far too many things that would lead people to reject me and my invitations.

Thankfully, my great redeeming God, who treats people better than you or I ever could, hasn't rejected me. He's the God of unlimited second chances who continues to talk to me, inviting me to a friendship with him—a friendship that can't help but change the way I talk to others.

He's the same God who invites you. Take him up on his offer. Drink deeply of his friendship and pass along what you experience of him to those around you, one word at a time.

General Index

Scripture Index